Ashvaghosha
The Awakening of Faith

This is the title of one of the most important religious books in the world, occupying, in the literature of the Higher Buddhism, a place not dissimilar to that of our own *New Testament.*

Its importance is increased when one considers that it formulates the fundamental doctrines of the Mahayana School, and was written by Ashvaghosha, one of the greatest poets of India, during the early part of the first century AD—a period when communication between East and West was reasonably frequent and extensive.

Not only have Buddhist sages considered it of the utmost worth—it has also been counted one of the five most valuable Buddhist scriptures by eminent Western scholars, and has been quoted and praised by such writers as Aldous Huxley, Dr. E.Y. Evans-Wentz (in his monumental Tibetan series published by the Oxford University Press), E.A. Burtt (Sage Professor of Philosophy at Cornell University), Christmas Humphreys, Maurice Percheron, Dr. Edward Conze, and others.

Should we decide to estimate the value of books by the number of those adhering to the doctrines expounded therein, then, after the *Bible,* the *Quran*, the Confucian Classics, and the Vedas, this volume ranks not only as one of the five most important books of Mahayana Buddhism, but fifth among the sacred books of the world.

Much published work offers material for a study of the apparently common ground of Buddhism and Christianity, but few shed greater light than this reasonably short work by the first and finest full-length biographer of Gautama the Buddha.

Dr. Timothy Richard, the translator of the work, was born in a small Welsh village in 1845. An excellent linguist, he won the prize for Hebrew early in his student days, and during 1868, while still at college, determined to visit China. Most of his life was spent working in that country, and he was deeply loved by all, from the meanest peasant to the Dowager-Empress herself. He died in 1919. His work has received the praise of eminent critics and scholars.

A.H. Walton

Alan Hull Walton was born in 1917, in Northumberland, and educated at The Royal Grammar School and Durham University. Before settling in a flat overlooking Hampstead Heath he travelled extensively, and visited France for lengthy periods. Described by one critic as "a medieval scholar set down in the present day," he possesses a library of over 6,000 volumes. He first came to notice during 1941, when his translations from the poetry and prose of Baudelaire were well received both here and abroad. His reputation was established by work in the fields of sociology, morals, and religion. He is also an expert bibliographer. We quote below from reviews of some of Mr. Walton's previous works:

"Mr. Walton knows what he is talking about. . . . A labour of love."

—Charles Morgan

"A veritable mine of information. . . . The author's treatment of such a difficult subject is beyond all praise. He has brought to the completion of this highly interesting volume unusual skill and literary ability."

—James Burnett, M.A., M.D., LL.B., F.R.C.P.

"His version is most successful. . . . "

—Michael Roberts

". . . is to be congratulated on the completion of an ambitious undertaking sure to earn him the gratitude of serious scholars. . . . He has written with a facility disclosing deep knowledge and understanding of the subject. The immense source material . . . is extremely well condense. In addition the author shows a ready knowledge of languages and mastery of English prose."

—Herman Goodman, B.S., M.D. (New York)

Ashvaghosha

The Awakening of Faith

Translated by
TIMOTHY RICHARD

Edited with an Introduction by
Alan Hull Walton

Foreword by
Aldous Huxley

Munshiram Manoharlal
Publishers Pvt. Ltd.

ISBN 81-215-1141-0
This edition 2005
First edition 1961

Typeset, printed and published by
Munshiram Manoharlal Publishers Pvt. Ltd.,
Post Box 5715, 54 Rani Jhansi Road, New Delhi 110 055.

Contents

Foreword

The enormous literature of Mahayana Buddhism is still very poorly represented in English translations, and most of such translations as have been made are now out of print or inaccessibly buried in learned journals.

The publishers of this new edition of the Richard version of *The Awakening of Faith* are to be congratulated on their enterprise in making available once more this important Mahayana text.

ALDOUS HUXLEY

Los Angeles
California, 1960

Introduction

I. General

The growing interest of the West in Buddhism, more particularly during the past fifty years or so, may be assigned to several causes. These have included the widening and expansion of our knowledge of Oriental religion and philosophy, the increasing availability, not only of scholarly studies and commentaries, but a growing choice of translations of the better-known texts, and the appearance for the first time, in translation, of hitherto little-known scriptures. Moreover, Victorian materialism having lost its corrupting grip, our Orientalists, scholars, philosophers, and psychologists have found an intense sympathy added to their intellectual curiosity in these matters. Much of this healthy change has been due to the work of scientists such as Eddington, Jeans, Schroedinger, and Einstein, and to that of psychologists such as Dr. Carl Jung of Zürich, who was the pioneer in bridging the gap between Chinese thought and Western psychology.

Scientists themselves have long felt that rationalistic philosophy, based as it is on a view of the world as studied by natural science, is undoubtedly inadequate,[1] and there have been many signs

[1]See, for example, *Science and Christian Belief* by C.A. Coulson, Oxford University Press, 1955 (and Fontana Books, London, 1958); *The Mysterious Universe* by Sir James Jeans, Cambridge, 1930 (reprinted in Pelican Books, 1937); *Science and Religion*: A Symposium, London, Gerald Howe Ltd., 1931 (this volume contains twelve essays revised by their authors from Broadcast Talks, and includes such writers as Sir Arthur Eddington. The Bishop of Birmingham, Julian Huxley, Dean Inge, Father O'Hara, H.R.L. Sheppard, Canon Streeter, and Sir J. Arthur Thompson). Also of interest is *The Universe and Dr. Einstein* by Lincoln Barnett, London, Collins (Comet Books reprint), 1956—see especially pp. 112-13, where Einstein's views on God are quoted.

Of considerable importance is *What is Life,* by Erwin Schroedinger, Cambridge University Press (1944, latest reprint 1955). In this connexion an interesting and valuable lecture by Dr. Griffith Evans, has recently been printed in *The Fourth International Conference on Divine Healing,* 1959, published by the London Healing Mission, 20 Dawson Place, London, W.2. The author is an adherent of Einstein and the "Unified Field Theory," and two brief quotations may serve to indicate a point of view which he elaborates in detail: "Someone protected in a recent number of *Mind and Matter* against religion being mixed up with this radiation theory—Max Planck and Einstein say they cannot be separated, because you cannot separate mind from matter at one pole nor from spirit at the other, and you cannot logically separate spirit from an over-ruling cosmic mind, intelligence, or whatever we like to call it, but the man in the street calls it God. . . ." "I think we could face the whole academic world from our premise of belief in God. We have contemporary prophets in Raynor Johnson and Douglas Fawcett. Only those who really since the beginning of the present century that the centre of gravity in religion is rapidly moving away from external authority to inward experience. The emergence of this trend was perhaps first implied by William James in his classic series of Gifford Lectures, *The Varieties of Religious Experience.* And Aldous Huxley, the most erudite of living writers in this field, combining the knowledge of the scientist, the perception of the psychologist, and the vision of the seer, has, in his profoundly important anthology and commentary, *The Perennial Philosophy,* given infinitely further ground for believing that the basis of genuine religion rests on inward experience, rather than on strict adherence

want to understand the spiritual because they believe in it, can do so. 'If with all your hearts ye truly seek Me ye shall surely find Me'—and you can find understanding in the language of Douglas Fawcett if you already *want* to find it."

Dr. Evans realizes that science is divided against itself in this matter because "the majority remain Newtonian . . . and most of those who control academic medicine are Newtonian; there is not a single book on wave-function in any of the central medical libraries in London. . . . They don't even keep the *Eddington Memorial Lectures*. . . ."

A further lecture by Dr. Evans is to be found (in French) in the periodical, *Le Portail,* numéro spécial, Février, 1958, pp. 115-20, published by R.E. Forget, Thonon-les-Bains (Haute-Savoie), 39 Avenue d'Evian, France.

It may be wondered why the word "healing" has crept into a footnote herein, but it is important to state that the work of such men as Dr. Evans is directly concerned with the relationship and compatibility existing between science, higher physics, and religion.

to orthodoxy and its outward ritual. This is the way of the mystic, and it is the way which Ashvaghosha leads us in the present work, the way to the inward experience of God.

Many times has the question been asked: "What is mysticism?" One of the simplest, and perhaps one of the clearest definitions, is that given by Evelyn Underhill: "Mysticism is the art of union with Reality. The mystic is a person who has attained, that union in greater or less degree; or who aims at and believes in such attainment."[1] The word "God" may be substituted for "Reality" if the reader prefers. Pfleiderer, for instance, says: "Mysticism is the immediate feeling of the unity of the self with God." And Pringle Pattison explains that "Mysticism appears in connexion with the endeavour of the human mind to grasp the divine essence or the ultimate reality of things, and to enjoy the blessedness of actual communion with the highest."

I am inclined to agree with Dean Inge that the mystical sense or faculty, so far from being a rare endowment, is almost universal in one form or another. The rarity lies not in the possession of a potential or scarcely developed faculty, but in the extremely limited number of those who speculate on its origin, or try to penetrate ever more deeply

[1]Evelyn Underhill, *Practical Mysticism*, London, Dent; New York, E.P. Dutton, 1914, p. 3 (in the original the passage is italicized).

into its secrets (the philosophic and the contemplative mystics respectively). This faculty, which does not explain itself, may be strengthened and deepened by cultivation, and those who have led the life of cultivation, seeking only the treasures of the spirit and the jewel of wisdom, are among the greatest benefactors of humanity.

It has sometimes been a habit, sometimes a fashion, to cast aspersions on the contemplative life. In our present age of big business syndicates, automation, hypnotic publicity, commercial television, ever-more-speed, newer-than-new, better-than-best, and thinly veiled regimentation—a society, in fact, *en pleine décadence*—there is every danger that such an attitude may become a duty. The answer to all such shallow and superficial attitudes is that voyages of discovery are made not only by a Captain Cook or a Christopher Columbus, but also by the sage, the savant, the philosopher, and the saint, who "voyage through strange seas of thought alone," and whose discoveries may be equally, and sometimes infinitely more far-reaching and beneficial in their results.

Often enough it has been claimed that mysticism is virtually the same in all countries, in all ages and places; that it is timeless, and independent of history. This is true, for the voyage has been mapped out in many countries, at different times, and by followers of dissimilar creeds; yet although the roads are various, there are so many correspondences between them we may be certain that they are described by those who have travelled along, and accurately noted, these ways. The aim, whether Christian, Buddhist, Sufi or Hindu, is always the same: "God Himself—the unchanging, eternal fountain of all being, the summit of all reality." (That is to say Union with God, Union with Reality, or with the One or Divine Mind—the terms may be interchangeable.) William James expressed it thus: "In Paul's language, I live, yet not I, but Christ liveth in me. Only when I become as nothing can God enter in and no difference between his life and mine remain outstanding."[1]

Among the Persian mystics Al-Ghazzali said, "The Science of the Sufis aims at detaching the heart from all that is not God, and at giving to it for sole occupation the meditation of the Divine Being." Therefore, the first thing to be aimed at is detachment of the mind from outer sensations, for these interfere with concentration, impede "atonement." Also implicit in the pronouncements and teachings of the mystics is the doctrine that eternity is timeless, and that if we "live in the eternal" our immortality is as much here and now as in the future. Moreover, it seems always to be understood that "if a man will seek the Good for anything beyond itself, he will never find it."

Asking the question "Is there a 'best' type of life?" Raynor Johnson describes a group of Indian

[1]William James, *The Varieties of Religious Experience*, London, Longmans Green & Co., 1907, p. 418.

contemplatives at a remote Himalayan fastness called Gangotri. "They are," he says, "engaged in exploring an inner world whose sublime heights and abysmal depths are more magnificent than those on which their outer eyes can look. . . . These men are not misanthropes, or ignorant of another kind of life: some have been to universities and some have taken part in public affairs. They have chosen to live thus—to forsake the comforts of the body and the companionship of friends, for a quest of the spirit."[1]

In the West we may find this difficult to understand, but in the growing interest in such (and allied) things there are signs that at last we are beginning to understand—that we may be commencing to reap something of the harvest sown by a few pioneers who, in the previous century, returned from the East with an unshakeable desire to make known in their own countries a philosophy and religion, not only venerable in its tradition, but one which remains a vital and dynamic force in those countries which follow its teachings. This has been shown by the increasing availability of reasonably priced translations and books on Buddhism; and, more recently, by the appearance in paper-backed editions of studies and translations

[1]Raynor C. Johnson, *The Imprisoned Splendour,* An approach to Reality, based upon the significance of data drawn from the fields of Natural Science, Psychical Research and Mystical Experience, London, Hodder and Stoughton, 1953, sec. edn., 1958, p. 407.

by eminent and distinguished scholars and translators.

The present volume may, therefore, be expected to reach a wider circle of readers than in time past, and a few remarks seem necessary. It must, however, be stressed that it is not possible in the course of a few introductory pages to deal in any adequate fashion with so profound a subject, nor to give detailed information on the history or doctrines of Buddhism, and the differing or conflicting points of view held by some scholars with regard to particulars.

As D.T. Suzuki, the learned authority on Zen Buddhism has said, this religion has completed a form which, in its later developments, distinguishes it from its so-called primitive or original type—"so greatly, indeed, that we are justified in emphasizing its historical division into two schools, Hinayana and Mahayana," or the Lower Path and the Higher Path of Salvation.[1]

[1]Suzuki speaks of the "Lesser" and "Greater Vehicles" of Salvation. W.Y. Evans-Wentz comments with reason as regards the translation of these words: "We have given preference to Sj. Atal Bihari Ghosh's rendering of *Mahayana,* of which he says: '*Mahayana* may, and possibly does mean, the 'Greater' or 'Higher Path' (or 'Voyage'), and *Hinayana* the 'Lesser' or 'Lower Path' (or 'Voyage'). *Ya* (of *yana*) means 'to go' and *yana* 'that by which one goes.' Western Orientalists have adopted 'Vehicle' as an equivalent of *yana,* . . . but 'Path' is preferable" (*Tibetan Yoga and Secret Doctrines,* arranged and edited with introductions and annotations by W.Y. Evans-Wentz, London, Oxford University Press, 1935; sec. edn., 1958, p. 1).

Suzuki goes on to say (*An Introduction to Zen Buddhism*) that the Mahayana, "with all its varied formulae, is no more than a developed form of Buddhism, and traces back its final authority to its Indian founder, the great Buddha Sakyamuni."

These two schools of Buddhism[1] are also geographically divided, the Hinayana (sometimes called Southern Buddhism) being common to southern India and Ceylon, etc., and the Mahayana (or Northern Buddhism) being common to northern India, Tibet, China, and Japan—where it attained a further development known as Zen.

It has been said that Gautam Sakyamuni expounded his principles to most of his followers in the more exoteric form of the Hinayana, but amongst the few enlightened and spiritual disciples capable of understanding and receiving such teachings, he transmitted them in the esoteric form of the Mahayana. Nevertheless, as Evans-Wentz has written, "An esoteric Buddhism thus conceived is not . . . to be regarded as in any wise in disagreement with canonical, or exoteric Buddhism, but as being related to it as higher mathematics are to lower mathematics, or as being the apex of the pyramid of the whole of Buddhism."[2] Another

[1]There are a number of sub-divisions or "sects," the differences of which cannot be entered into here.

[2]Evans-Wentz, *The Tibetan Book of the Dead,* London, Oxford University Press, 1957, pp. 5-6. The first edition appeared in 1927, and subsequent editions have been enlarged. Later editions contain a long Psychological Commentary by Dr. C.G. Jung.

difference between the two schools has been pointed out by Waddell, who draws attention to the Mahayana substitution of a theistic doctrine (and a pantheon of emanations), in place of the almost agnostic idealism and simple morality of the Southern School.[1] He claims, however, that even the Southern School shows a "considerable leavening with Mahayana principles."

The chief distinguishing marks of the Mahayana are its organized and hierarchical priesthood, not unlike that of the Christian church, together with its forms of ritual and worship, its doctrines complicated by esoteric and "transcendental teachings," its emphasis on yoga, its belief in Bodhisattvas, and its full acceptance of a Primordial Source of all Being—the Adi-Buddha (Adibuddha).

The more primitive Southern Buddhism contains little comparable to this. Its priests are only very loosely organised, nor is there any recognised Ruler of the "Church" such as the Dalai Lama, or God-King of the Northern Buddhists. Its ritual cannot be compared with that of the Higher Buddhism; and the only Bodhisattva found in its temples, and

[1]Waddell, *The Buddhism of Tibet*, Cambridge, Heffer, 1895; latest reprint 1959, p. 10. Waddell's book needs to be read with care. It is a voluminous mine of information, but his attitude is that of the Victorian materialist, and he incorrectly refers to certain aspects of Buddhism as "nonsense," "gibberish," or "stupidity." And had he been speaking of Christianity would most likely have referred to the Miracles in the same spirit.

prayed to, is Maitreya, or the "Coming Buddha" (in Pali: *Metteya*).[1] As is well enough known, Gautama himself committed none of his teachings to paper, and for very many years after his death they were passed down in a faithful oral tradition, as was Christianity. It seems undoubted that the principal organiser in the practical dissemination of Primitive Buddhism was not Ananda, the favourite pupil of the "Blessed One," but another of his disciples, Sariputra, who, after hearing the Master, left everything to follow him, and, thus, received enlightenment in his turn. This man was tremendously erudite, and gifted with a pre-eminently analytical intellect. He organised the tenets and doctrines in such a way that any and everybody could study, understand, and remember them with ease. Hence, the exoteric aspect of the Hinayana.

The basic ideas of the Mahayana are set forth in what is known as the *Prajnaparamita* group of literature,[2] and it is claimed that the earliest of these were set down about three hundred years after Gautama's death. In essence they doubtless belong

[1]Maitreya is the "Loving One"—the Messiah of Buddhism, who will redeem the world through Divine Love at the end of the present *kaliyuga*, or "Age of Darkness." His will be the age of universal peace and brotherhood between men, such as that which Christ has promised.

[2]An excellent selection from this enormous series of writings has been translated by Dr. E. Conze, *Selected Sayings from the Perfection of Wisdom*, London, The Buddhist Society, 1955.

to Primitive Buddhism; but their development was not possible until the followers of the Buddha had actually lived his teachings for a period, and under the varying and changing conditions of life.

In contradistinction to the Hinayana, the Mahayana teaches that man is not able to avoid the continuing cycle of earthly rebirths by practising the method of Gautama alone (austerity, chastity, desirelessness, non-attachment, etc.). As Percheron has explained, it is essential to seek one's refuge in the Buddha, but it is also necessary to "turn one's soul towards some power capable of helping and saving; in other words, to appeal to divine mercy; and joined to this support, to make use of it so as to attain for oneself the wondrous state of the compassionate saviour."[1] Thus, the Hinayana is the School of Salvation by Works, and the Mahayana the School of Salvation by Faith in Bodhisattvas (or Saviours). A final distinction between the two schools has been set forth by the Tibetan saint, Milarepa, in his *Jetsun-Kahbum*, as set down by Rechung: "I have understood that one who aimeth at his individual peace and happiness adopteth the Lower Path (the *Hinayana*). But he, who from the very start, devoteth the merit of his love and compassion to the cause of others, I understand belongeth to the Higher Path (the *Mahayana*). To leave the Lower Path and to enter upon the Higher

[1]Maurice Percheron, *Le Buddha et Le Boudhisme,* Paris, Editions du Seuil; London and New York, Longmans Green and Co. Ltd., 1957 (English translation by Edmund Stapleton).

Path, it is necessary to gain a clear view of the goal of one's aspirations."[1]

Signs of the emergence of Mahayana teachings had been evident about 200 years BC, but they were not formulated and expounded with clarity until the reign of Kanishka, during the first century AD, when Ashvaghosha sent them forth into the world, later to be developed by the great commentators, Nagarjuna, Asanga, and Vasubandhu.

Of Ashvaghosha himself little can be said. The various accounts of his life are contradictory, and so much legend has been added that it is difficult to decide where imagination ends and truth begins. What follows, however, can be taken as factual.

He was a Brahmin later converted to Buddhism, travelling extensively in central and northern India, and was contemporary with—and possibly adviser to—the Scythian King, Kanishka (Kanerkes). He was one of India's greatest poets, and besides *The Awakening of Faith* left other works, even of which were translated into Chinese.[2] Timothy Richard retells the story of his conversion as follows: "The day had come for a public discussion on religion, as was common in India at that time, and Ashva-

[1]Evans-Wentz, *Tibet's Great Yogi Milarepa*, London, Oxford University Press, 1928 (sec. edn., 1951), p. 140.

[2]His celebrated *Life of the Buddha* (the *Buddhacarita*) was translated by Beal. A condensed version has been translated by Dr. Conze in *Buddhist Scriptures*, Penguin Classics, 1959, where he describes it as "the first, and in may ways the finest, full-length biography" of Gautama, p. 34.

ghosha and Pareva were to be the debaters. Ashvaghosha said, "The one unable to answer shall have his tongue cut out." The other replied, "No, he shall become a disciple of the winner." Then he asked Ashvaghosha, "What shall we have to do in order to keep the kingdom in perfect peace, to have the king live long, to let the people enjoy abundance and prosperity, all free from evils and catastrophes?" Not being able to answer this, Ashvaghosha became the other's disciple.

II. The Awakening of Faith

The *Mahayana-Sraddhotpadashastra* is the title of one of the world's most important religious books, and has been translated as: *The Awakening of Faith*. It could also be translated as: *The Mahayana Faith*, or *The Faith of the New Buddhism*. As the present translator claims, it is not only Brahministic and Buddhistic, but Indian and Western in some of the aspects of philosophic thought which it presents; and on occasion there are analogies with the thought of Hegel, Berkeley, and Gore.

No Sanskrit copy is known to exist, but the work was translated into Chinese *circa* AD 557 by the Buddhist Missionary Paramartha (also known as Kulanatha), with the aid of interpreters and scholars of the Liang Dynasty, chief among whom was the celebrated Chinese philosopher, Chi-chi.[1]

[1]See also *infra*, p. xxxvi of this Introduction.

Ashvaghosha teaches, as has already been implied (*supra*, p. xx), that Salvation is attained, not by doctrinal belief, behaviour, or the following of ritual, but by treading the Higher Path in the way of Spirit and of Truth, and with selfless compassion for all sentient beings. The main theme of his book is that Mind is the sole reality, that it is One and Indivisible; yet the One manifests itself in the many, the Macrocosm cannot be separated from its Microcosms, nor can they have any real existence apart from each other.

This is to say that the universe, the world, and everything in it, have no absolute existence. Their existence is merely relative, and all concrete tangibility and visibility is merely illusion. All things are but a reflection, a shadow cast by Reality, and only unenlightened sentient beings perceive them as permanent solid things existing in themselves. Modern science bears this out, and a Doctor of medicine can say today: "As to the concept of *matter* one which we base our everyday actions, its apparent solidity has been proved an illusion of our sense-organs. It comes about in a manner roughly similar to the illusion of solid objects in three-dimensional moving pictures: as a result of electronic processes which take place in practically empty space. The space occupied at any given moment by electrons is less than the billionth part of the most solid object perceived by our senses. . . . Not only is the solidity of the body an illusion, but also the theory that the electronic pattern behind it is maintained by rigid laws of nature. . . . This means that the constancy of the book in front of you is maintained by the fact that in spite of the unpredictable behaviour of many of the electrons composing it, the majority fills always the same place."[1] Matter exists only as phenomena, and is, thus, a development, a reflection of thought—the Thought of Cosmic or Divine Mind, which is the One,[2] and which might accurately be described as a crystallisation of mental energy. This was the view expressed by Sir James Jeans: "If the universe is a universe of thought, then its creation must have been an act of thought. Indeed the finiteness of time and space almost compel us, of themselves, to picture the creation as an act of thought. . . . Modern scientific theory compels us to think of the creator as working outside time and space, which are part of his creation, just as the artist is outside his canvas. It accords with the conjecture of Augustine: *Non in tempore, sed cum tempore, finxit Deus mundum.* Indeed, the doctrine dates back as far as Plato. . . ."[3] . . . and earlier, if we travel

[1]Gotthard Booth, "Science and Spiritual Healing" in *Religion and Health.* A symposium edited by Simon Doniger, New York, Association Press, 1958, pp. 66-67.

[2]There being only One Mind, and man being in, of, and created by that One Mind, when he thinks, he himself uses it—but being gifted with free-will, he can use it for good, indifferent, and, as we too often realise, for diabolic ends. Sorcery, in fact, may be described as the reasoned use of this Infinite Mind to achieve purely finite ends.

[3]Sir James Jeans, *The Mysterious Universe,* Penguin Books (Pelican series), London, 1937 (and reprints), pp. 182-83. See also pp. 168-69, and 186-87.

farther East. Elsewhere Jeans has said, "We have not seen the addition of mind to matter so much as the complete disappearance of matter, at least of the kind out of which the older physics constructed the objective universe."[1] These views have been stressed at length by Evans-Wentz in the Introductions to his monumental Tibetan Series: "From the standpoint of Western Science, particularly of dynamics and physics, the One Mind is the unique root of energy, the potentiality of potentialities, the sole dynamo of universal power, the initiator of vibrations . . . whence there come into being the cosmic rays and matter in all its electronic aspects. . . . It is thus . . . the architect of the atom and the builder therewith of world systems. . . ."[2]

Such knowledge was given utterance in the Occident by Plotinus (*c.* AD 203-62), and the *Enneads* of this important mystic, though voluminous, will amply repay study.[3]

[1]*The New Background of Science*, Cambridge, 1933, pp. 283-84.

[2]*The Tibetan Book of the Great Liberation*, London, Oxford University Press, 1954, p. 9. (This volume contains an extremely long introduction of the utmost value in the present connexion, as well as a Psychological Commentary by Dr. C.G. Jung.)

[3]There are few complete translations of Plotinus English—or any other language. The best by far is that of Stephen MacKenna, *The Enneads*, translated by Stephen MacKenna, second edition revised by B.S. Page . . . with an Introduction by Professor Paul Henry, S.J., Faber and Faber, London, 1956. The reader should also refer to *The Philosophy of Plotinus* by W.R. Inge, London, Longmans, 1918.

The One Mind, the Cosmic Mind, the Divine Mind, whether of Buddhist, Neo-Platonist, or Christian Mystic, are, as Aldous Huxley has clearly demonstrated,[1] one and the same. This idea of the One and Infinite Mind is perhaps more simply expressed by the Mental scientists,[2] and is to be found, for example, in the verbiage of Mary Baker Eddy, where it forms the basis on which Christian science has been built, and built on a rock which is firm and sure.[3] In this concept matter is but the shadow reflected by Mind. In his study of Mrs. Eddy[4]

[1]*The Perennial Philosophy*, London, Chatto and Windus, 1946 (and many reprints—and now available in England as a paperback in the Fontana series published by Collins).

[2]See, for example, *The Edinburgh Lectures* by Thomas Troward, New York, Dodd, Mead and Company, 1909 (and many reprints). Also Ralph Waldo Trine's *In Tune with the Infinite*, of which there are many editions (London, Bell & Co.); and *The Power of the Silence* by Horatio W. Dresser, London, Gay and Bird, 1901. These last two authors were highly esteemed by William James. With regard to Dresser, see*The Varieties of Religious Experience* (London and New York, Longmans, 1907 edn.), p. 96, text and footnote 1. A new edition is now available as a paperback, London, Collins, Fontana Library, 1960. Mention might also be made of a simpler work: *Your Mind Can Heal You*, by Frederick W. Bailes, London, George Allen & Unwin, 1942, etc. (this volume obviously originated from America, although its author is an English medical man).

[3]The philosophy of Mary Baker Eddy, which undoubtedly has analogies with Buddhism, is most succinctly expressed in her "Scientific Statement of Being" on p. 468 of *Science and Health with a Key to the Scriptures*, ll. 8-15.

[4]Lyman P. Powell, *Mary Baker Eddy, A Life Size Portrait* London, Nisbet & Co., 1930 (printed in the USA), pp. 107-8.

Lyman P. Powell (not a Christian scientist, but an orthodox clergyman) says, "As for the nothingness and erroneousness of matter, this is an idea almost as old as human thinking. Before ever Gautama took his seat beneath the Bo-tree, India was accepting it as a general concept. As early as 430 BC Democritus of Abdera remarked, 'Man lives plunged in a world of illusion and deceptive forms which the vulgar take for reality'."

Thus, the Buddhist does not investigate the essence of matter, but concerns himself only with those sense-perceptions which give rise within us to the idea of matter. So-called objective reality held little of interest for Gautama, except in a relative sense, and he defined the world "as that which appears as world within our consciousness."[1] Finally, although Mind is One and Indivisible, the All in All, that aspect of it which mediates between "the universal and the individual-intellectual consciousness is the spiritual consciousness, which takes part in both sides. It represents the stabilising element of the mind, the central point of balance, upholding the coherence of its contents by being the centre of reference. But for the same reason it is also the cause for the conception of egohood in the unenlightened individual, who mistakes this relative point of reference for the real and permanent centre of his personality."[2] Thus, the Mahayana

[1]Lama Anagarika Govinda, *Foundations of Tibetan Mysticism*, London, Rider & Company, 1959, p. 66.

[2]Ibid., p. 74.

does not deny the objective and subjective world, but points out that this illusory existence of separateness becomes the opportunity for defilement when discriminated in the direction of dualism. To awaken faith and reach enlightenment—and to avoid illusion—it is necessary to still the mind and "one" oneself with God.

III. Buddhism and Christianity

In his original Introduction to this translation, the Reverend Timothy Richard, suggested, as had several scholars, that the Mahayana Faith was "not Buddhism, properly so-called, but an Asiatic form of the same gospel of our Lord and Saviour Jesus Christ, in Buddhistic nomenclature, differing from the Old Buddhism just as the New Testament differs from the Old." He gives several reasons for this, adding that "both Christianity and the New Buddhism hold to the transcendent and the immanent forms of God," drawing attention to the age-old intercommunication between East and West, and the existence of Nestorian Missionaries in the Far East from a very early period.

This theory has been disproved so far as basic doctrines are concerned, for the writings of Ashvaghosha are evidence in themselves that the Mahayana was essentially the same during the first century AD as it is now. There may have been some Christian influence at a later period, but it was slight. It is much more likely, due to intercommunication between the far East and the West, that

Christianity was somewhat influenced by Buddhism—and those religions which preceded Buddhism. It is significant that in its earliest days Christianity accepted the doctrine of reincarnation.[1] Origen, St. Augustine, and St. Francis of Assisi subscribed to it.

Much later Marco Polo admires the austerity of Buddhist monks, and compares Buddha to a Christian saint,[2] but this does not imply that either religion was responsible for any profound influence on the other; though the fact that there may have been some influence both ways seems very possible. According to Huc,[3] Tsong-Kha-pa, who reformed the Tibetan Buddhist Church in his establishment of the Ge-lug-pa during AD 1407, was influenced by Roman Catholic priests who had settled near the place of his birth. And there is also the earlier tradition regarding the journey of St. Thomas the Apostle to India.

Certainly the exponents of the Mahayana—especially in its Tibetan form—were very willing to ponder the wisdom embodied in religions other than their own, and have never assumed a defensive

[1]See Leslie D. Weatherhead, *The Case for Reincarnation*, London, City Temple Literary Society, 1957.

[2]R.E. Latham, trans., *The Travels of Marco Polo*, Penguin Books (Penguin Classics), Harmondsworth, 1959, pp. 256-57ff. References are also made to St. Thomas the Apostle on pp. 238, 248-49, and 278.

[3]Huc, *Travels in Tartary*, translated from the French by W. Hazlitt, two vols., London, *c.* 1850.

or offensive attitude against those who do not accept their creed or outlook—as the Lama Anagarika Govinda recently pointed out during a memorable broadcast. In this they are unique.

The Analogy between Buddhism and Christianity remains, and it cannot be denied that Christianity appropriated the story of Gautama in the devotional tale of the conversion of the son of King Josaphat by the Christian monk, Barlaam.[1] With regard to the similarity of doctrines there remains the possibility of Buddhist influence on Hellenistic and Essenian groups, for about 250 BC, King Ashoka, a great power in earlier Buddhism, had sent missionaries to several places in the West, including Egypt and Syria. The first mention of Buddha in a Greek text does not occur, however, until two hundred years after the commencement of the Christian era, in Clement of Alexandria.

But, whatever the explanation of the similarities may be, students of these religions will find that each of them teaches the way of meditation, contemplation, and union, and each expresses itself in a consuming and tender desire to assist all men and women attain the goal of salvation.

IV. Nirvana

The aim of Buddhism, as of almost every other religion in the civilised world, is to show the way and the means by which the transcendent state of

[1]By St. John Damascene; translation available in the Loeb Classics.

the unconditioned can be attained. But no Buddhist doctrine has been so much misunderstood as that of *nirvana,* which is the "State of the Unconditioned." This is a term the implications of which are very difficult to describe, and which defies precise definition in words. Translated literally it means: "the blowing out," as of a candle, or "becoming cool" with regard to sensuous experience. It has also been mistranslated as "total annihilation." This has been responsible for the Western conception of Buddhism as an atheistic philosophy, when in reality it is a theistic religion.

Correctly understood, the word should be interpreted as the disappearance of the "Three Fires of Desire"—Lust, Ill-Will, and Stupidity. In the transcendent or supreme state of *nirvana* these are replaced by Purity, Good-will, and Wisdom and result in the Perfect Knowledge of Buddhahood. Thus, the Tibetan translation from the Sanskrit of *nirvana, is mya-nan-med*, or "The Sorrowless State;" for Lust, Ill-will, Stupidity, and the illusion of worldly pleasure, are the cause of sorrow.

Nirvana is the opposite of the *samsara,* or this worldly world of illusion in which we live, and which is recognised by such scientists as Jeans, Eddington, Rayner Johnson, and others, as being illusion. Burt defines it as the state achieved by the conquest of craving, the spiritual goal of Buddhism; but this is not enough. Humphries more clearly defines it, briefly, as a state of supreme enlightenment beyond the conception of the intellect—the annihilation of all we know as the personal, separative self (*Buddhism*, Pelican Books, 1951, 1952, 1954, etc.). It is the attainment by the indivi-dual one of unity with the All-embracing One, and, unlike the Jewish and Christian Heaven, it is not the final abode of the immortal soul, nor yet a condition of spiritual absoluteness. It is the State of Perfect Enlightenment, attainable not necessarily after the decease of the body, but also here on Earth whilst in the flesh—this being the aim of contemplation, meditation, and non-attachment, as in yoga. It is the realisation that there is no duality, that *nirvana* and the *samsara* (the world of manifestation, of illusion, of "becoming"), that time and eternity, are indistinguishably one. It is neither "being" nor "non-being," and, as such, it is not intellectually realisable; nor is it conceivable by the unenlightened. Yet it has been realised by the great yogins and Buddhist saints, as by Plotinus, and the Christian saints and mystics, such as St. John of the Cross, St. Theresa of Avila, the anonymous author of *The Cloud of Unknowing*, and Jacob Boehme.

Like the Divine Ground of all Being it is indescribable by finite mind, because it transcends all the concepts of finite mind. It is complete spiritual enlightenment, or the realisation of the Mind in its True State. Just as the experience of the mystic, it can be known, but not described. Thus, as Aldous Huxley has said, Gautama "declined to make any statement in regard to the ultimate divine reality. All he would talk about was *nirvana*, which is the name of the experience that comes to the totally selfless and one-pointed' (*Perennial Philosophy*, Chatto and Windus, London, 1954, p. 56). Eliade puts it thus: "*Nirvana* can be 'seen' only with the 'eye of the saints'—that is, with a transcendent organ which no longer participates in the perishable world."

The Heaven of the orthodox Christian is an abode of eternal bliss in which the liberated soul resides eternally. The *nirvana* of the Buddhist is the timeless spaceless unity of the One. It is the state temporarily relinquished by the Bodhisattva, in order that he may manifest in the *samsara* to work, incarnate, for the salvation, not only of man, but of all sentient beings.[1]

V. The Translation and its History

Timothy Richard, the translator of the work which follows, was born at Ffaldybrenin, a small village in Carmarthenshire, in 1845. About the age of sixteen he felt a strong call towards religion, and in 1865 entered the Haverfordwest Theological College in Pembrokeshire, where he proved a brilliant student. Excellent as a linguist he early won the prize for Hebrew. During 1868, while still at college, he determined to go to China, and for this purpose applied to the Baptist Missionary Society. He was accepted in the spring of 1869, and sailed from Liverpool in November of the same

[1]See *infra*, note, p. 4.

year. Almost the remainder of his life was spent in China, where his work brought him into close and very friendly association with the ruling powers. Convinced of the necessity for diffusing throughout that country a knowledge of the humanitarian principles of the West, he devoted not only his own purse, but most of his spare time to giving educational lectures, greatly arousing the interest of the Mandarin class. Eventually he was instrumental in founding the University of Shansi. His conception of the meaning of "The Kingdom of God" urged him to ceaseless work for the uplift of the whole man, body, mind, and spirit, and for this he was deeply loved by all, from the ordinary peasant to the Dowager-Empress herself. In token of appreciation for this work and influence for good over the people, he received the highest official honours which China could bestow, and privileges rarely there accorded to foreigners. He died in 1919.[1]

His literary work includes a translation into Chinese from the *Introduction to the Devout Life of St. Francis de Sales,* a partial translation from the Chinese of the *Hsuan Fo P'u* (*Guide to Buddhahood*), as well as a translation of a work by Wu Ch'êng-ên under the title of *A Mission to Heaven* (more recently

[1]See *Timothy Richard of China,* by W.E. Soothill, London, Seeley, Service & Co., 1924; *Forty-five Years in China* (Richard's Autobiography), London, Fisher Unwin, 1916; and *A Maker of Modern China,* by A.J. Garnier, London, The Carey Press, 1945, etc.

translated by Arthur Waley as *Monkey*). Richard's contribution to the study of Buddhism, his conception of an ultimate "Eternal Buddha who is life," has resulted in a deeper understanding of Mahayana Buddhism as distinct from that of the Hinayana. He may not always have been strictly accurate in the literal sense, but, as Soothill has shrewdly pointed out, "his imaginative sense carried him into regions beyond the reach of other eyes, for vision leaps over chasms, leaving plodders to build bridges for feet to tread. To reveal a new point of view is the work of a prophet, and—to every man his gift!"

As stated *supra*, p. xxii, the original Sanskrit texts of *The Awakening of Faith* were lost centuries ago—as were many other Buddhist works written in that language. Two Chinese translations had, however, been made: one in AD 557, by Paramartha, and another about AD 700, by Çikshananda, who was also a Buddhist Missionary in that country.

Richard worked from the Paramartha version, and in 1900 Teitaro Suzuki published (at Chicago) a translation he had made from the Çikshananda text.

Richard's work originally appeared at Shanghai, in 1907, and at Edinburgh in 1910, but is now extremely rare. Quite apart from its interest for the scholar and theologian, this particular version seems admirably suited to those readers with a Christian background, yet who lack more than a slight acquaintance with Buddhist thought.

His discovery of Ashvaghosha and his translation of the work are described by Richard as follows:

"In 1884 I visited Nanking in company with my revered friend David Hill, to see the Viceroy, and to persuade him to interest himself in securing religious freedom for Christians and immunity from persecution. Whilst there, I sought for some Buddhist books which I could not procure in the north of China. I learnt that a Buddhist Book Society has been started in Nanking, Suchow, and Hangchow, three of the leading cities in central China, in order to replace those destroyed during the Tai Ping Rebellion. Of the three societies, the most important was that at Nanking, and the prime mover of the whole three societies lived there. His name was Yang Wên Hui. I called on him, and found him the most intelligent Buddhist I had ever met. He had been several years in Europe as treasurer to the Chinese Embassy when Marquis Tseng represented China in England and France. Mr. Yang had had interviews with Max Müller and Julien and Bunyiu Nanjio of Tokio, who had studied under Max Müller. Thus, besides being well acquainted with the Buddhist authorities in China, he was personally acquainted with the best authorities in Europe and Japan. Mr. Yang was not a Buddhist priest, but a Confucianist with the B.A. (Siutsai) degree, and was only a lay Buddhist.

"I said to him, 'How is it that you, with a Confucian degree, should have ever become a

Buddhist?' His answer was striking: 'I am surprised that you, a missionary, should ask me that question, for you must know that Confucianism shirks some of the most important questions. It only deals with human affairs now, not with the superhuman.' 'But do you mean to say that Buddhism answers these questions?' He said, 'Yes.' 'Where?' I asked again. He answered, 'In a book called *The Awakening of Faith*. That book converted me from Confucianism to Buddhism.' 'Have you got that book for sale here?' I asked. 'Yes,' he replied, and brought the book and laid it in my hands. Finding him to be most thoroughly conversant with the relative value of the various Buddhist books, I asked him to select for me some dozen works which he considered most important. Having paid for them, I returned to my inn. Shortly after, the box containing all my purchases arrived. I looked for the book on *The Awakening of Faith*, and began reading it, and sat up till the small hours of the morning. I cried to my friend Hill, who was also sitting up late at work, 'This is a Christian book, and most interesting.' 'Christian?' my friend cried, with great doubt. 'You are reading your own thought into the book!' 'Well, then,' I said, 'how do you explain these passages?' pointing to some to which there was no ready explanation.

"Three months later I was in a bookseller's shop in Edinburgh, and looking through his new books, I came across Beal's little book on Buddhism, then just published. Turning up a certain chapter in it, I found that he referred to *The Awakening of Faith* as a pseudo-Christian book which it was desirable to have translated!

"Years passed by. In 1891 I was transferred to Shanghai. Shortly after, I met my friend Mr. Yang again, and I told him that I had read *The Awakening of Faith* with great interest, but that frequently I came across philosophical terms, which no existing dictionary explained, and which even excellent Chinese scholars could not explain. If he could spare some of his time to come to Shanghai, I would spare some of my time to translate it with his help. He readily agreed, and was delighted to have the book made known to those interested in Buddhism in the West. Thus, the book was translated into English in 1894. But it was not published then, as I wished to have leisure time to revise it before publication. That time of leisure has never come. Six years later (1900), Suzuki's translation into English was published by the Open Court, Chicago. His translation bears the mark of one who has spent much study on the subject, but he did not possess the knowledge of the true key to the fundamental and central idea of the whole book, namely, Chen Jû. He translates it by 'Suchness,' which obscures his whole translation;[1] whereas I

[1]Personally I feel that "Suchness" is the preferable translation, but this may be because I am so used to it myself. I have heard it said that Suzuki eventually became dissatisfied with his translation, and would not allow it to be reprinted. —A.H.W.

give the literal translation. True Model, meaning God, which later I found confirmed in an old standard Buddhist work called *Wan Fa Kwei Sin Luh*. In Suzuki's Introduction, he quotes a large number of different authorities about Ashvaghosha. But as he approaches the subject from the non-Christian point of view, the light which comes from a comparison between it and Christianity is denied him. He dwells more on his philosophical 'Suchness' or on his psychological theory of 'triple personality,' and only on one religious characteristic 'faith,' apparently unconscious of its incalculable importance as a religious eirenicon between the East and the West. Though I have had no time to carefully revise this translation of mine, I publish it because I believe it is capable of producing brotherhood amongst men of different religions, when interpreted in the light of Christianity."

VI. The Editing

Richard's translation, in which he was assisted by an able Chinese Buddhist, and for which he made continual reference to commentaries on the work, has been left as he wrote it—with the following exceptions. The term *Tathagata* has been substituted for his *Ju Lai* (which he considered might sometimes best be rendered "messiah" in English). The term *Bodhisattva* has likewise been substituted for his *Pusa*, or *Pusa* saints. This brings his version more into line with other translations made from Mahayana scriptures. A footnote has been added *infra*, pp. 4-6, for the benefit of the general reader (the original edition is without notes), and a few small faults and some errors in punctuation have been corrected.

It has been felt that the text was otherwise best left alone, for Richard has been quoted by various authorities on Buddhism—more particularly by Dr. Evans-Wentz in his Tibetan series—and most readers will necessarily wish to refer to his exact wording.

One Chinese term which offered some difficulty was *Chen-jû* = true so, like. In Sanskrit this would be translated as *Bhutatathata: Buta* (= chen) = true, and tathata (=*jû*) = so, like. In Sanskrit it means Reality, all existence, whilst in Chinese it is usually interpreted as substance, qualities, and immutable law, the universe, or the universal. Suzuki has translated it, justifiably, as "Suchness," which is the "Quality of the Void." Other possible interpretations are "Thusness," "The Cosmic Order," the sumtotal of all factors which shape the universe, the norm of existence, the womb in which all things take their shape and from whence they are born. Richard has translated this term in various ways—*True Form, True Likeness, True Reality, Archetype, True Model,* and so on. Occasionally, *True Reality* has been substituted for Richard's *True Form* or *True Model,* etc.

With these remarks we leave the reader to the text, of which its translator said, "If we estimate the value of books by the number of adherents of their doctrines, then, after the *Bible*, the *Quran*, the Confucian Classics, and the Vedas, this volume, about the size of the gospel of Mark, ranks next, or fifth, among the sacred books of the world."

ALAN HULL WALTON

Highgate, London, 1960

The Awakening of Faith

Opening Hymn

I yield my life to the All,
To the All Soul, full of good,
In wisdom all complete,
In power all divine,
In pity—would save all.

To Law which does embody
The Archetype of all.

To Church which does contain
The Archetype in Seed,

That men may be delivered
From doubt and evil ways;
Get Faiths in the Great School
Perpetuating God!

Chapter 1

Reasons for Writing the Book

Question 1: What are the reasons for writing the book?

Answer: The reasons for it are eight:

A. Generally speaking, it is to induce all living beings to depart from the way of all sorrow and to obtain the highest happiness, instead of seeking the glitter of fame and the wealth of this world.

B. It is to make clear the fundamental idea of the incarnate God (*Tathagata*) in man, and to lead all beings in the right way, avoiding error.

C. It is to lead these ripe in goodness to continue in the Mahayana Faith without failing.

D. It is to enable those in whom the root of goodness is very small to cultivate faith more and more.

E. It is to show how to remove evil hindrances and to strengthen well the mind, to keep far from mad pride, and to see through the deceits of vice.

F. It is to show how to study and correct the errors of ordinary men and the errors of the two inferior schools (the Hinayana or elementary school and the Madhyi-yana or middle school of Buddhism).

G. It is to show the means by which one may ascend to the abode of God (Buddha) and never lose faith.

H. It is to show the benefits of this Faith and to exhort men to practise it.

There are the main reasons for writing this book.

Question 2: As the Sutras, or classic Buddhist Scriptures, explain these things fully, what need is there of repeating them?

Answer: Although the Sutras have discussed these things, yet as men's abilities and attainments are different, the reception of instruction is necessarily different. When the incarnate God (the *Tathagata*) was on earth, all men were able to understand him. His body and mind far excelled those of all other men. When he delivered his perfect words, all living beings, though different in kind, understood him alike, and, therefore, there was no need of explanation.

But after the *Tathagata*'s death we find that some men, after widely reading our Sacred Scriptures, have the power unaided to understand them; we find that others, after only hearing a little of the Sacred Scriptures, have the power unaided to understand much; we also find that some have not sufficient intelligence to understand the Scriptures unassisted by extensive explanations; whilst we find that others dislike voluminous writings and prefer a terse style which embraces many principles, and which they are able to understand.

Thus, this book is written for the last class of men which desire to know the general principles of the great and profound Law of the *Tathagata* with its infinite applications.

CHAPTER 2

The Fundamental Doctrine of the Mahayana Faith[1]

Having explained the object of writing this book, we now proceed to consider the fundamental doctrine of the Mahayana Faith. The great school (Mahayana) speaks of the Eternal Soul of the

[1]The following brief definitions of some terms used in Buddhist sacred writings may be useful to readers not fully acquainted with this terminology. Fuller information may be found in the works listed in the bibliography at the end of the book.

Bodhisattva: A Bodhisattva is one who has vowed to work for the benefit of all sentient beings (not for *man alone*, as in most religions); for he is concerned not only with his own salvation, but with that of all living creatures, and works towards this end by realising Perfect Enlightenment. The word may be translated as "Great Teacher," or even—in a sense only—by the Christian word, "Saint." The first aim of the Bodhisattva is to bring about, within himself, the destruction of all sensuality and worldly attachment; and having achieved this state of Enlightenment and Purity, he universe, His nature and His attributes.

A. By His nature is meant the Soul of all living beings. The soul embraces that of saved and of unsaved beings, and it is this universal Soul that characterises the great school. For it is the Archetype's True Eternal Form which is the nature of the Mahayana Faith; and the Archetype's temporary form in life which is able to make manifest the nature, form, and use of the Mahayana Faith.

B. As to the attributes of the Soul, they are three. The first is the vastness of its nature.

renounces entry into *nirvana* in order to teach others the Truth of Perfect Enlightenment, thus, bringing them on the path which leads to Buddhahood.

According to his vow, he will enter *nirvana* only when all creatures in this world, and in others (i.e., the state known as Hell), have attained salvation and deliverance from the *Sangsara* (*Samsara*), or world of illusion and unreality (i.e., the earthly life, and, thus, the antithesis of *nirvana*). This teaching implies that Evil will eventually be transmuted into Good, and so the eternal damnation of the Semitic and Christian religions finds no place in the Mahayana. The early Christian writer, Origen (martyred in AD 254), also held the view that everlasting damnation was not compatible with the all-embracing and everlasting love of God, who is All Good. According to Harnack (*Das Wesen des Christenthums*), Jesus felt similarly about the sick and the sinful—he never asked if the sick person deserved to be healed, for he knew from the Father that all manifestations of the kingdom of Satan had to be overcome.

Thathagata (in Chinese, *Ju Lai*): One of the titles of Gautama, the Buddha. According to Humphreys it may mean: "He who follows in the footsteps of his predecessors." Conze has it:

All things are originally one and the same and an eternally fixed quantity in the True Model. The second covers its vast manifestations. In the person of the *Tathagata,* the True Model Come, there are infinite possibilities stored up as in a womb. The third is its vast power. It is able to produce all good among all classes of unsaved beings.

All the enlightened Buddhas follow this Mahayana Faith, and all the Bodhisattvas attain to the perfection of Tathagatahood by the methods, of this Faith of the New Buddhism.

"He who has thus come," adding, "as the other Buddhas have come." It also means "The Perfect One."

Kalpa: This word means an epoch of time, an age, or vast period in time.

Amitabha: The Buddha of Infinite Light, who has the Wisdom of Discrimination, of Clear Vision. He is, thus, the Buddha of "inner vision," of meditation and spiritual discernment. The "inner eye" and "inner vision" seen by that eye correspond to him. He is the personification of that Discriminating Wisdom by means of which the religious man is enabled to know each thing separately, yet all things as One. He is the Buddha of meditative visualisation which leads to ultimate integration, known in Japanese as *amida*. His cult was clothed having inaugurated by Saraha, who was master of Nagarjuna, the great Buddhist teacher of the second century BC, who founded the Madhyamika, or Middle-School.

Paramita: Simply described as "Perfection," or "Ideal Virtue" this term needs fuller explanation. In the Mahayana there are six *Paramitas*, each representing a stage of spiritual perfection achieved by the Bodhisattva on his journey to Buddhahood. In some forms of Buddhism the number of *Paramitas* is extended. [A.H.W.]

CHAPTER 3

Expositions of the Mahayana Faith

These expositions are of three kinds:

A. Those about the meaning.
B. Those about the correction of erroneous conceptions.
C. Those about the different steps of progress.

As to the meaning of the One Soul, there are two aspects:

1. One is the eternal transcendent Soul.
2. The other is the temporary immanent Soul.

These two aspects embrace everything, for they are really one.

1. THE ETERNAL STATE OF THE SOUL

The Soul or Mind of the True Model is the great essence of the invisible and the visible worlds. As to the nature of this One Soul, it is the same in all forms. To think it is different in different forms is only a false notion of the world. Once we penetrate beyond forms, it is discovered that all the different forms of the universe are not real differences of soul at all, but different manifestations of one real power, hence, it has always been impossible to speak adequately, to name correctly, or to think correctly of this One Soul, the real essence of things, which is unchangeable and indestructible. We, therefore, name it the "True Essence or the True Likeness or the True Reality or Model." But all nomenclature of these matters is imperfect, and if one follows superficial thought, the true meaning cannot be found out. Even though we call it the True Model, it has no form. It is because language in its extremity fails us that we coin a new term to avoid ordinary ideas. But the nature of this Archetype is a reality that cannot be destroyed, for all things are true though they cannot be truly pointed out to the senses, and all forms are really only different manifestations of the one True Model. It should be remembered that this is beyond ordinary language and beyond ordinary thought, therefore, we name it the True Model.

Question 3: How then are men to follow and obey and find the way to this True Model of things?
Answer: One must know that although one cannot speak of this adequately, as it is beyond all expression, and although one cannot think of this adequately, as it is beyond all thought, yet we call this state the seeking after; and that when we leave ordinary thought of these things, we are entering into the gate of knowledge. Next, when using

words to discuss the True Model, it may be spoken of in two ways, namely, first as the unreal as compared with ordinary realities, in order eventually to show its reality; secondly, as the only real as compared with ordinary realities, because it has a nature of its own full of infinite possibilities.

A. (Ia) *First, then, the Unreal*

When we speak of the unreal, we mean that which has never been defined, which is separate from all existing forms, and which common men cannot understand.

We should know the nature of this True Model. It has no form, yet it is not formless. This is not saying that it is without any form, but that it is not the ordinary form. It is composed of neither ordinary, existing, nor non-existing forms. It is neither one definite form nor is it the many different forms. This is not saying that it has no definite form and that it is not in the many different forms. It is neither one nor many different forms. Generally speaking, as the world has many different notions, all false, we call this the Unreal Empty Form. But if false notions are given up, this is then the most Real.

(Ib) *Secondly, the Real*

When we speak of the Real, we have already explained that the True Reality is apparently Unreal but true; in other words, that it is the true mind, eternal, and uncharged, full of purity, therefore, we call it the Real One. But it has no form. When the imperfect notions of things are given up, then alone can we verify this truth.

2. The Eternal Soul Immanent in the Temporary

The temporary arises from the forces of the Eternal *Tathagata*, the uniting of the eternal with the temporary. It is neither the same nor different, but we call it the Natural state of man. This natural state has two meanings, namely, that which embraces all things, and that which produces all things; the first is called the Infinite Enlightenment, the second the Finite Enlightenment.

(IIa) *Infinite Enlightenment*

By infinite enlightenment is meant that which has no false notions and is infinite like space, one with the True Reality, as in instinct and intuition. This is the natural state of the Incarnate True Model (the *Tathagata*), and is called the original state of enlightenment. This is to distinguish it from acquired enlightenment, which cultivates that infinite enlightenment, for the two have the same thing in common though it is only in part. Where there is the original infinite enlightenment there exists finite enlightenment in those who seek after it. Where there exists finite enlightenment, there is more enlightenment to be acquired.

Again, when one attains to the original enlightenment, it is called the perfect enlightenment. When one has not attained to the original enlightenment, it is not perfect enlightenment.

For example, when an ordinary man discovers that his former ideas were wrong, and is able to prevent such ideas arising anymore, such knowledge on his part, though it might be called a kind of enlightenment, is only finite.

Or when those learned in the wisdom of the two lower schools (the primary and secondary, or smaller and middle) or such Bodhisattvas as are beginners in the Mahayana school are enlightened so as to know that there is in one sense a difference, and in another no difference between these two classes of ideas, we call their knowledge partial enlightenment.

Or when those, such as the saints who have arrived at different stages of attainment, are enlightened to know that there is in one sense a resting-place and in another sense no rest, in order to distinguish things more clearly, their knowledge is called partial enlightenment.

Or when the saints have arrived at the highest attainment with all the means of deliverance completed and their thoughts are exactly in accordance with the original enlightenment, and they are enlightened to know that when the false notions began, these had no real beginning; then they escape far from the microscopic anxious thought to things, for they are able to see the true nature of the One Mind. This state is the eternal one which we call the perfect enlightenment. Therefore, the Sutra says that when one can apprehend that which is behind thought, one is on the way to Buddhist wisdom!

Again, as to the beginning of imperfect notions in the mind of men, these have no beginning. But when we speak of their beginning, we mean that they arise without thought, therefore, are not called enlightened, as they have not exercised thought. As each thought has been transmitted without interruption from the beginning, and men's minds have not been able to free themselves from this, the imperfect notions have been said to be without beginning and to be finite enlightenment. If we meet a man without these thoughts, we shall then know the different stages in the development of the mind, such as beginning, resting satisfied, considering, ending, because without thought he knows that there is really no difference in kind between the enlightened neophyte's enlightenment and the original enlightenment. For the four states are co-existent and not independent, but are originally all alike—different stages of one and the same enlightenment.

1. Next, original enlightenment in men appears according to the different degrees of confusion in two different states, but not separate from the original enlightenment. These different states are the state of pure wisdom and the state of unspeakable blessing where things are incomprehensible.

(a) The state of pure wisdom is that which exists when, under the transforming influence of the True Model, cultivating one's nature according to the True Model till all departments of deliverance are completed, one reaches the state where the temporary gives way to the eternal and is grafted on to the Eternal Mind, manifesting itself in the three spiritual institutions—of Buddha (Godhead), of Law, and of Priesthood, hence, called the perfect and pure wisdom, because all who are dependent on the senses alone are unenlightened. Those in the unenlightened state do not depart from the nature of enlightenment; they are neither destructible so long as they depend on the original enlightenment nor indestructible when independent of that. Just as the water in the ocean, on account of wind, forms itself into waves, wind and waves being inseparable, and yet motion is not an attribute of water (for if the wind ceases the waves also cease), but the fluid nature of water remains indestructible; so the true nature of man is a clear pure mind. Though on account of the rise of the wind of finite enlightenment the pure mind is moved, the pure mind and the finite knowledge in man's heart are unseen and inseparable, but this mind's nature is not finite enlightenment. If the finite enlightenment ceases, then the imperfect notions will cease, and the wise nature remains indestructible.

(b) The state of unspeakable blessing is practical, when it follows pure wisdom and is able to do all sorts of wonderful things, being called the state of infinite blessings, unceasing and natural. In proportion to the natural goodness it abounds in all kinds of blessings according to the need of all.

2. Next consider the attributes of this enlightenment. They are four, and great, infinite as space and clear as a mirror.

(a) Infinite light of the Eternal (Real Emptiness). It is very different from all thought and form. It cannot be made apparent and enlightenment cannot reveal it to the unenlightened.

(b) Infinite light of energy which influences things and which is called the unseen forces (not Real Emptiness). All appearances in the world are brought about by this. They are without appearing and disappearing, without loss or destruction, eternal in the One Mind. All existence is but the true nature of this Mind. Moreover, no kind of defilement can defile this. Its wisdom remains unchanged, full of perfect energy, influencing all men.

(c) Infinite light of the law of deliverance called the invariable law of Salvation (not Unreal Law), which sets aside the hindrances of pessimism and the hindrances to ordinary wisdom and leads one out of the state where the mortal and the immortal are combined so as to attain the perfect free light of life.

(d) The infinite light of practice, called deliverance according to the law, shining on the minds of all living beings, leading them to practise goodness by methods suitable to their needs.

(IIb) *Finite Enlightenment or Acquired Knowledge*

This is not like the knowledge of the Eternal that

there is only one way: hence, finite enlightenment shows itself in many forms of existence. These forms have not independent existence separated from the original enlightenment. Just as with a man who has lost his way, his losing of the way depends on his original knowledge of his course (for if he had no idea of the way at first, he could not be said to have lost it), so with men, it is because they have the idea of enlightenment that they know they are unenlightened. If they had no idea of enlightenment in the abstract, they could not be said to be altogether unenlightened. From imperfect ideas of unenlightenment men are able to understand the meaning of words and true enlightenment. If we dispense with finite enlightenment, we cannot conceive of true enlightenment.

1. First, finite enlightenment may be viewed in three ways always inseparable from it:

(a) *Sensation*. When the unenlightened mind is excited we call it sensation. When there is enlightenment there is no excitement; if there is excitement there is pain, as effect follows cause.

(b) *Consciousness*. This occurs when following any excitement one becomes conscious of something. Without sensation there is no consciousness.

(c) *Perception*. This is formed when following consciousness the external becomes real. Without consciousness there are not perceptions of outside objects.

Since there is an objective world, there arise again six aspects of it according to another classification, namely:

(i) *Consciousness*, which arises from outward objects which the mind distinguishes one from another—discriminating between what it likes and what it dislikes.

(ii) *Emotion*. This follows consciousness and produces joy and sorrow. These false ideas arise from constant partial enlightenment.

(iii) *Attention*. This follows emotion, reaching after everything, seizing on joy and sorrow, and cleaving to them with the whole mind.

(iv) *Conception*. This follows perception, distinguishing it by giving it a name.

(v) *Will*. This follows the giving of names to things in all sorts of action.

(vi) *Discrimination*. This is the result of different action, and is inevitable. We should know that unenlightenment can produce all kinds of false methods, because they are within the state of unenlightenment.

2. Next, infinite enlightenment and finite enlightenment may be viewed together in two ways, where they are the same and where they are different.

(a) As to where they are the same. Take, for example, the various kinds of pottery: they are all made of one clay. In the same way finite enlightenments are manifestations of the One True

Essence, and the Sutras according to this doctrine say that all things are eternal and divine. Perfect enlightenment cannot be cultivated or made, can never be added to, and has no form which can be seen. That which has form to be seen accompanies useful transformations. It is not the nature of real Wisdom, for this Wisdom is invisible.

(b) As to where enlightenment and unenlightenment differ, it is like speaking of the different kinds of pots made. Infinite enlightenment and finite enlightenment differ according to their useful transformations, and the infinite nature appears different in the transformations.

3. Next, the finite forces which control human nature, such as the changes of mind and consciousness, arise from ignorance and unenlightenment. They may be seen manifested in our feelings and spoken of as mental powers. These mental powers have five names. One is the faculty exercised when in the midst of ignorance finite consciousness begins. The second is the faculty used when the mind takes note of something. The third is the faculty used when all phenomena are put in the objective. Just as outward things are reflected in a mirror, so does this faculty reflect what the five senses show instantaneously at all times. The fourth is the faculty used when distinguishing between the pure and impure. The fifth is the faculty used when it reflects impressions from one object to the other incessantly. It retains, the past infinite manifestations of one's own existence

with all their good and evil; it ripens into the knowledge of the causes of present and future joy and sorrow which are the unfailing results of our deeds; it is able to call up the past, lay it instantly before our mind, and to call up our finite knowledge of the future. Therefore, the phenomena of the three worlds (of desire, of form, and of no form) are mind-made. Without mind, then, there is practically no objective existence. Thus, all existence arises from imperfect notions of our mind. All differences are differences of the mind. But the mind cannot see itself, for it has not form. We should know that all phenomena are created by the imperfect notions of the finite mind, therefore, all existence is like a reflection in a mirror, without substance, only a phantom of the mind. When the finite mind acts, then all kinds of things arise; when the finite mind ceases to act, then all kinds of things cease.

Next, the faculty of thought. This comes out of the fifth as above. In common men this is very strong. The consciousness of self and of environment and all the imperfect ideas arising from these, trying to distinguish between all the objects of the senses, is called thought, and is also called the independent faculty, as well as the faculty of distinguishing things. This increases with the senses, with desires, and with their sorrows.

4. As to the origin of imperfect knowledge working in the finite, common men cannot understand this; nor can the wisdom of the two lower schools understand it; only the Bodhisattvas of

Higher Buddhism, when they begin to get right faith, and when they can examine things properly and test the nature of the True Reality, can understand it. Spiritual men can obtain a small insight into this; but even the higher saints when they have attained to their perfect state cannot understand the whole of it. Only Buddha (God) understands all. The mind from the beginning is of a pure nature, but since there is the finite aspect of it which is sullied by finite views, there is the sullied aspect of it. Although there is this defilement, yet the original pure nature is eternally unchanged. This mystery only Buddha understands.

When we speak of the original nature of the mind, eternally without thought, we call it eternally unchanged. As the human mind originally does not know the True Model, the mind does not correspond with the outward universe. They thought suddenly begins and is called the finite thought.

Confusion from correspondence with the objective. One can be delivered from this confusion by the two lower schools and be kept far from it in the station of full faith of the great school. Confusion arises through feeling corresponding with the objective. One can gradually avoid this by the cultivation of the means of deliverance in the full faith of the great school; by the cultivation to the First station in the pure state of the mind, all the confusion will be gone. (To understand these and the stations below, see *Guide to Buddhahood*, translated by the author.)[1]

Confusion through knowledge of differences by correspondence with the objective. By means of the second stage of separateness from the world, and by means of deliverance in the Seventh station, confusion will be gone.

Confusion through objective forms not corresponding with one another. By means of the Eighth station of freedom from form (or the immovable) and the confusion will be gone.

Confusion through subjective perception not corresponding with objective. By means of the Ninth station, when the mind is free (in holy wisdom) the confusion can be got rid of.

Confusion through subjective sensation not corresponding with the objective. By means of the complete Ten stations of the saints one may enter the state of Tathagatahood, Buddhahood, and be delivered from this last of the confusions. As the finite mind does not comprehend the Universal Soul, it begins by the correspondence of faith to examine into things and to rid itself of confusion. In its progress towards purity of mind, it step by step gets rid of confusion, and when it arrives at the state of Tathagatahood it is able to be free from it altogether.

The meaning of correspondence is that the finite mind's ideas of the universal True Form differ according to their stages of confusion or enlighten-

[1]*Hsuan Fo P'u*, Shanghai, 1907.

ment, and that the perfected finite knowledge and the outside universe are exactly the same. The meaning of want of correspondence is that the finite mind is unenlightened and has never known these differences, and that its knowledge and the outside universe are not the same.

Again, the confused mind is a hindrance to thought and darkens the original wisdom of the True Reality. Ignorance is called the hindrance of wisdom, and darkens the natural wisdom of the world. What does this mean? It means that, owing to the confused mind, its perceptions, its objects and thoughts are not in accordance with the Eternal Nature. It means that, owing to the universal True Form being eternally at rest, without being finite or temporary, ignorance and unenlightenment differ from the eternal, therefore, they are unable to follow the perfect wisdom of all the universe.

5. Next the finite state. This is of two kinds. First, the rough, ordinary state, when it corresponds with the finite mind. Second, the fine extraordinary state when it does not correspond with the finite mind. There is also the lowest of the ordinary, such as the state of common men, and the highest of the ordinary. There is, too, the lowest of the extraordinary, such as the state of the Bodhisattvas; and the highest of the extraordinary, such as the state of Buddha. These two kinds of the finite state arise from the different extent of the influence of ignorance. As to cause and effect, the cause is unenlightenment, the effect is the manufacture of

a false imperfect world. If the cause is removed, then the effect is removed. If the imperfect cause ceases, then the imperfect mind which does not correspond with the real universe also ceases. If the result ceases to be erroneous, then the mind which corresponds with the real universe also ceases to be erroneous.

Question 4: If the finite mind ceases, how can there be continuation? If there be continuation, how then do you speak of finally ceasing altogether?
Answer: What is destroyed is only the finite state of the mind, not the mind's being, just as wind in relation to water is a moving power. If there be no water, the effect of the wind is not apparent; there is nothing to show it. If the water remains, the state of the wind is made apparent; only when the wind ceases does the moving of the water cease. It is not the water that ceases to exist. So ignorance in relation to the True Real Nature is made apparent.

If there were no True Real Nature of the mind, then all existence would not exist; there would be nothing to show it. If the True Real Nature of the mind remains, then finite mind continues. Only when the madness of finite mind ceases will the finite mind cease. It is not the Wisdom of the True Reality that ceases.

6. *Influences*. There are four influences—the confused and the pure—incessantly at work. The first is a pure influence called the True Real One. The second is the cause of all confusion, called ignorance. The third is the confused mind, called

sensation. The fourth is the false world as known to the senses and called the objective.

Influences may be, thus, illustrated. Clothes have no scent, but if anyone smoked them with incense, the clothes would then be perfumed like the incenses. So it is with influences. The True Reality is pure and has really no confusion colour-ing it, but ignorance in man colours his views, so that there is a confused state. The confusion caused by ignorance has really no true purity, but the True Reality influences the mind, so that there is an effort after the true purity.

(a) How is it that confused influences are acting incessantly? It is in relation to the True Model that there is ignorance as a cause of the confusion. This ignorance colours the True Model in the finite mind. As there is an influence at work, there arise false imperfect ideas, and these colour the True Model again so that one does not understand it. Unenlightenment then arises, bringing a new world of false conceptions on account of this result. These false ideas in turn colour other false conceptions again, causing the mind to be fixed of these, and to desire to do all sorts of things, incurring, thus, all kinds of trouble of both mind and body.

(i) The influences of the false objective world are of two kinds; namely, those which arise from increased thought, and those which arise from increased action.

(ii) The influence of the false imperfection of faculties are of two kinds; namey, those which arise voluntarily from faculties producing the highest saints of the lower school (the Hinayana), the highest saints of the middle school, and the highest saints (Bodhisattvas) of the advanced school (the Mahayana), causing them to suffer the sorrows of life and change; and those which arise involuntarily from faculties producing ordinary men and causing them to suffer the sorrows of successive transmigrations.

(iii) The influences of ignorance are of two kinds: first, those which arise from the very root of things—intuition—which give rise to imperfect sensation; and second, those which arise from the senses and desires, and which give rise to imperfect impressions.

(b) How is it that pure influences are acting incessantly? It is because there is a True Model able to influence the ignorant, a power at work causing man's misguided mind to dislike the sorrows of transmigration and to seek the joys of divine rest (*nirvana*). As this ignorant mind is moved to dislike transmigration and love *nirvana*, this fact influences the finite mind to believe that its nature is finite and to know that its finite mind is full of false ideas; and further, that there is no true objective world before men, and that, therefore, they are to cultivate some way of deliverance. As from the True Model man knows that there is no objective world, then the various means of following and obeying this True Model arise spontaneously (without thought and without action); and when influenced by this power for a long time, ignorance disappears. As ignorance disappears, then false ideas cease to arise. When false ideas cease to arise, the former objective world also ends. As the forces cease to exist, then the false powers of the finite mind cease to exist, and this is called *nirvana*, when the natural forces of the True Reality alone work.

(i) The influence of the imperfect mind is of two kinds, namely, that which arises from positiveness and literalness, as in common men and in those of the two lower schools, causing them to dislike the rounds of transmigration and, according to their strength, to gradually move towards the unsurpassed way of Buddhism; and that which arises from the five faculties of the mind, where the higher saints start to copy the True Model to reach *nirvana* quickly.

(ii) The influence of the True Model, which is of two kinds, namely, that which arises from subjective influences of the True Model element itself, and that which arises from outward conditions.

(I) The influence of the True Model itself is from eternal ages, having infinite resources complete with benefits beyond all thought. It underlies the nature of all phenomena.

On account of this twofold aspect the power of these influences is increasing, causing all men to dislike the sorrows of transmigration and seek the joys of *nirvana*, believing that in their own persons there is the influence of the True Model, and that, therefore, they have a mind to cultivate it.

Question 5: If this be so, that all living beings have the True Model in them, and that all will be equally influenced, why should there be the infinite distinction of believing and unbelieving, some first and others later? Should not all at the same time know the power of the True Model, causing them to diligently cultivate the means of deliverance, and enabling all to enter *nirvana*?
Answer: The True Reality is originally only one, but the degrees of ignorance are infinite, therefore, the natures of men differ in character accordingly. There are unruly thoughts more numerous than the sands of the Ganges, some arising from ignorant conceptions and others arising from ignorance of senses and desires. Thus, all kinds of wild thoughts arise from ignorance, and have first and last infinite differences which the *Tathagata* alone knows.

Again, in the method of all the Buddhas there are means of utilising their forces. The nature and the means must be at work to be complete. Just as wood, though it has fire latent in it (this fire being the real force), cannot burn unless men know this and use means to call it forth, so with men although there is the power of the influence of the True Model in them, if it does not meet with the noble forces of the Buddhas and Bodhisattvas as means to call it forth, there would be no means of preventing wild thoughts, and, thus, of attaining *nirvana*. And although there would be the force of outward conditions, yet without the influence of the True Model there would not be the power by which one could discard the sorrows of transmigration and seek the joys of *nirvana*.

If the forces and the means of utilising them are complete, such as the force of the influences of the True Model, and also of the loving vows of the perfected Buddhas, and of the almost perfect saints to save the world, there arises a dislike to sorrow and a belief in *nirvana* and the cultivation of a good character. When the good character is attained, such people find the Buddhas and Bodhisattvas teaching them directly the benefits and the joys of the doctrine, and they are able to enter into the way of *nirvana*.

(II) The influence of outward conditions. This is the power of outward forces, and these outward conditions are incalculable. We indicate two kinds, those of different methods and those of the same spirit.

(i) As to the influences of different methods, they are those which operate when men follow the Buddhas and the Bodhisattvas from the beginning of their desire to seek truth till they themselves become Buddhas, and which influence them all through their course, be it in what they see or think, whether through their own family, parents, or relatives or through servants, or dear friends, or through enemies, or by means of the four attractions (such as those caused by alms, kind words, help and sharing in toil), even including all sorts of incalculable means, in order to set in action the power of the loving influences of the Buddhas and Bodhisattvas, so as to induce all beings to increase in goodness and benefit by what they see or hear. These means are also of two kinds, namely, the direct, which enables one to get saved quickly; and the indirect, which enables one to get saved after a longer time. The direct and indirect means are again of two kinds, namely, the progressive practice and the final attainment.

(ii) As to influences of the same spirit, all the Buddhas and Bodhisattvas desire to deliver all men from sorrow, and these spirits influence men constantly without ceasing, and they are of the same nature and wisdom and power, therefore, manifest the same spirit in all their experience. This is experienced when men in their ecstasy are able to see the Buddhas.

(III) The different between the influences of the True Model is of two kinds. The first is the uncorresponding. It is that of the common man or of the two lower schools and first stages of the Great School. These are influenced by their consciousness and impression, but are able to improve by means of the power of faith. They have not attained to that correspondence of mind with the Absolute whereby they are one with the nature of the True Reality, and have not attained that experience which is natural and perfectly corresponding to the work of the True Reality.

The second is the corresponding. It is that of the perfected Buddhas who have attained to the state when their mind is not different from that of the True Reality, but corresponding to the nature and work of all the Buddhas. In this state men are able to act naturally by means of the power of Absolute Spirituality, and by the influence of the Absolute to put an end to ignorance.

(c) Next note the confused state.

The influence of this confused state has been going on from eternity without ceasing, but when one reaches the state of Buddhahood this ceases. But the influence of the pure state has no end; it has an eternal future! It is the influence of the Absolute Reality. The confused idea is ended, and the spiritual is manifested in the influence it exerts on work, and has no end.

7. As to the nature and state of the Absolute, that of all common men, that of the lower school, that of the middle school, that of the advanced, and that of the Buddhas are without a difference, only having more or less of it. It is neither that which had an origin sometime, nor that which will end at sometime; it is really eternal. In its nature it is always full of all possibilities, and is described as of great light and wisdom, giving light to all things, real and knowing. Its true nature is that of a pure mind, eternally joyful, the true soul of things,

pure, quiet, unchanged, therefore free, with fullness of virtues and attributes of Buddha more numerous than the sands of the Ganges; divine, unending, unchanged, and unspeakable. It is most complete, without lacking anything, it is called the treasury or storehouse or womb of the *Tathagata* (the Model Come), and also the Divine Body of the *Tathagata*.

Question 6: Now you have said above that the nature of the Absolute is the same in all beings and is apart from all forms, how is it that you speak of its nature as having all these different possibilities?

Answer: Although real and possessing these possibilities, yet they are not different qualities; they are of one kind only, one Absolute Reality; there is a likeness in all the different manifestations, therefore, they cannot be different. Again, how do we say that there is a difference? It is in relation to consciousness and the finite that this difference appears. And how does it appear? As regards the origin of all things there is but One Mind, not an unenlightened Mind conjecturing at things. But in the finite there are imperfect ideas. The unenlightened mind begins to think of the world around, and this we call ignorance. If this finite thought conjecturing at things had not arisen, there would have been great wisdom and light. When the human mind begins to see that there exists the unseen beyond, where the mind nature is independent of this seeing, then it finds that this unseen shines throughout the universe. If the mind is excited or prejudiced, the knowledge is not true knowledge. When it has not found its true nature, it is not eternal, not joyful, not the true soul of things, not pure, but is busy and decaying, and, therefore, not free, and thus full of confusion more numerous than the sands of the Ganges. On the other hand, if the mind is not excited or prejudiced by imperfect ideas, all sorts of pure possibilities more numerous than the sands of the Ganges are open to it. If in the human mind there arises an idea to be followed, it is because there is something lacking in the mind. Thus, the incalculable possibilities of the pure Absolute Nature is that of the One Mind. There is no need to think out any new idea; it is complete, and is called the divine state, the treasury or storehouse or womb of the *Tathagata*.

8. As to the work of the True Reality—it is that which is in all the Buddhas and the *Tathagata* from that first moment of great love and desire to cultivate their own salvation and then to save others, to the time of their great vow to save all beings throughout all future endless *kalpas*. They regards all living begins as their own selves, though they are not the same in form, for in reality all living beings and themselves are manifestations of the Absolute Reality without any difference; then with the aid of this great wisdom of the True Reality they put an end to ignorance, they see the divine, and there arise naturally all sorts of unimaginable

service like that of the Absolute Reality reaching everywhere. Yet these beings are not ordinary forms, for the Buddhas and the *Tathagata* are perfect embodiments of the divine. The chief thought is that they are not the ordinary ideas of the world; they are not ordinary workers, but such workers as influence or inspire people in their experiences, hence, we say they are the work of the True Reality.

(a) This spiritual work of the True Reality is of two kinds. The first is dependent on the senses (positive and literal) and on what the mind of the ordinary man and those of the two lower schools understand by them, hence this kind is called the common stage, as these people do not know that their work is the manifestation of their sensation, so regard it outwardly by colour and size, but do not fully know.

(b) The second is dependent on the faculties. It is what all the Bodhisattvas from the time they reach the first station till they reach the highest station have experienced, and is called the inspired stage. This stage has incalculable manifestations; these manifestations have incalculable states, and these states have incalculable blessings.

The results of this stage have also all kinds of incalculable glories according to their manifestations. They are endless and infinite, without measure, ever present in their reactions, indestructible, and never lost. These blessings are the results of the prefect influences of the six means of salvation (*Paramita* or Wisdoms) and of the transcendent influences of the Absolute Reality. Thus, the Bodhisattvas are full of immeasurable joy, hence, they are called the inspired spirits.

(c) As to what common men see, it is only the rough outline. These men according to their observations see all sorts of different living creatures in the six kinds of beings (gods, men, *asuras*, devils, hungry ghosts, beasts); they have not attained the state of joy, hence, they are called common spirits.

(d) As to what the Bodhisattvas know from the beginning of their free ideas, and what begins to appear to them by full faith in the True Model, they know some of its characteristics, and glory that they are ever present, immeasurable, only manifest in the mind, and inseparable from the Absolute Reality. But these Bodhisattvas still have some imperfect notions remaining, as they have not reached the full Divine State. If they reach a purer state of mind, and if they progress till they have reached the utmost state, the inspired is seen to perfection.

(e) When they pass beyond the sense and faculties, there is no visible state, for the Divine Soul of all the Buddhas has no outward form by which they are to be seen.

Question 7: If the Divine Spirit of all the Buddhas is separated from form, how can it manifest any forms?

Answer: This Divine Soul is the essence of all form, therefore, it can manifest itself in form. This is why we say mind and matter are eternally the same. As the essence of matter is wisdom, the essence of matter is without form and is called the embodiment of wisdom. As the manifested essence of wisdom is matter, it is called the all-pervading embodiment of wisdom. The unmanifested matter is without magnitude; according to the will, it can show itself throughout all the universe as the immeasurable Bodhisattvas, immeasurable inspired spirits, immeasurable glories, all different, without magnitude and without interference with one another. This is what ordinary senses cannot comprehend, as it is the work of the True Model (Absolute Reality).

9. Now we show how to proceed from the finite to the infinite. This is called analysing all experience of matter to mind. In all the six objects of sense there does not exist false conjectures as men's thoughts are. As the mind has no form, we seek for it at all points of space in vain. Just as a man having lost his way calls the easy west, although the East and West have not really changed, so is mankind lost in ignorance, calling the mind of the universe his thoughts! But the Mind is what it ever was, all unchanged by men's thought. When men consider and realise that the Absolute Mind has not need of thoughts like men, they are then following the right way to reach the Infinite.

B. *The rectification of Erroneous Conceptions*

All kinds of erroneous conceptions arise from our own conceptions of things. If we could put away these personal conceptions, there would then be no false ones. These personal conceptions are of two kinds, namely, false conceptions of the person as the self, anthropomorphically, and false conceptions arising from that.

1. That which regards personal being as self.

According to common language, it is of five kinds:

(a) Hearing the Sutras saying that the eternal nature of the *Tathagata* is in the end only vacuity like space, some men, not knowing that this expression was used in order to destroy belief in phenomena as real, say that Space or Emptiness itself is the *Tathagata*. How is this to be rectified? Men are to understand that space is nothing. It has not existence and is not a reality. It is a term in opposition to reality. We only say this or that is visible in order that we might distinguish between things. All phenomena are originally in the Mind and have really no outward form, therefore, as there is no form, it is a mistake to think there is anything there. All phenomena only arise from false notions of the Mind. If the Mind is independent of these false ideas, then all phenomena disappear. This is called the true glorious nature and wisdom of the *Tathagata*, the Model Come (manifested), and not mere empty space.

(b) Hearing the Sutras saying that the nature of

all things in the world is unreal, even the final nature of *nirvana* and of the True Model (the Absolute Reality), therefore, they are also intangible and eternally independent of all forms, some men, not knowing that it was for the purpose of destroying belief in phenomena that these expressions were used, say the nature of the True Model and *nirvana* is nothing but unreality. How is this to be rectified? They are to understand that the divine nature of the True Model is not unreal. It is full of infinite possibilities.

(c) Hearing the Sutras saying that the treasures of the *Tathagata* (the Manifested Model) are eternally fixed without addition or subtraction, and are potentially full of all possibilities, some men, not understanding it, say the treasures of the *Tathagata* contain both the distinctions of mind and matter. How is this to be rectified? According to the True Model, there is no distinction between mind and matter; it is on account of the defilement of the finite in the round of life and death that these distinctions appear.

(d) Hearing the Sutras saying that all the defilements of life and death exist because they are in the treasury of the *Tathagata*, as nothing is independent of the True Model, some men, not understanding it, say the attributes of the *Tathagata* originally contain everything that there is in the world pertaining to life and death. How is this to be rectified? As the attributes of the *Tathagata* from eternity only contain pure possibilities more numerous than the sands of the Ganges, they are not independent of the True Model. They never fail, and are not different from the True Model. As to the defilements of the world, they are all false; they have no reality behind them. From eternity they have had nothing in them corresponding to the *Tathagata*. If there had been defilement in the nature of the *Tathagata*'s attributes, to get rid of defilement by causing men to unite with the *Tathagata* would be an absurdity.

(e) Hearing the Sutras saying that life and death depend on the treasures of the *Tathagata*, and that *nirvana* also depends on the treasures of the *Tathagata*, some men, not understanding it, say that all beings have a beginning, and as they have a beginning they then say that the joys of *nirvana* which the *Tathagata* has obtained have an end when he comes again incarnate. How is this to be rectified? As the treasures of the *Tathagata* are without a beginning, so is the state of ignorance without a beginning. If it be said that beyond the three worlds—earth, heaven, and hell, or form, desire, and no-form—there are other beings, this is but the talk of non-Buddhist Scriptures. Moreover, as the treasures of the *Tathagata* are without an end, so is *nirvana*, which all the Buddhas obtain, without end.

2. To meet the intelligent of the two lower schools, the *Tathagata* only spoke to them of the True Model as not like men (not anthropomorphic). As he had not spoken fully to them of the temporary nature

of experience, they feared the rounds of life and death and sought a false *nirvana*. How is this to be rectified? As the nature behind all experience has no beginning, so it has no end—this is the true *nirvana*.

3. Finally, to leave false conceptions, one should know that purity and defilement are both relative terms and have no independent existence. Although all things from eternity are neither matter nor mind, neither infinite wisdom nor finite knowledge, neither existing nor non-existing, but are after all inexpressible, we nevertheless use words, yet should know that the *Tathagata*'s skilful use of words to lead men aright lay in this—to get men to cease conjecturing and to return to the Absolute Reality, for the best human thought of all things is only temporary and is not Absolute truth.

C. *Different steps of Progress*

These are the paths which all the Buddhas have passed through, and the goals reached by the Bodhisattvas when they have made up their minds to practise religion. Briefly speaking, religious growth or progress involves having three things: first, growth of perfect faith; second, growth in intelligent practice; third, growth in attainments.

1. The progress of perfect faith. It depends on the kind of man, and the kind of character he has, whether he gets a perfect faith worthy of progress. This again depends on uncertainty of character, whether tending to good or evil. If influenced by

goodness, believing that good and evil have their respective recompense, if able to abound in all sorts of good works, if tired with the sorrows of life and death, if desiring to obtain the highest wisdom by meeting all the Buddhas and by worshipping and supporting them in person and practising faith long under all conditions, then faith is perfect, and the Buddhas and Bodhisattvas teach such how to progress. Some, moved by great pity, are able to progress of themselves; others, on seeing the right doctrine about to be attacked, are moved to defend it. Such persons are able to progress. Thus, when faith is perfect and the religious aim is fixed, they enter the ranks of the upright and true fixed ones; they never go back, and are reckoned among the seed of the children of the *Tathagata*, being one with the right eternal cause of things.

(a) If the root of goodness in man be small, in the long run worldly affairs are like thick weeds choking it. Although these people should begin worshipping and supporting the Buddhas, they only become the seed to be born in a better state among men or in the abode of the lower gods, or may become the seed of the two lower schools of Buddhism, or may cultivate the great school. But goodness is uncertain—it may have taken root or may not. Or if men serve the Buddhas, though they have not served them very long, yet, on account of going through special circumstances, they also may strike root and grow. This will only be if they regard the Buddhas in a special manner. Or if they also learn from the followers of the two lower schools, they also may grow. On account of following the example of others, they also may grow. Those progressing for these latter reason are all uncertain. When they meet adverse circumstances, they fall back from the highest Faith to the two lower ones.

(b) Next, what is the progress of perfect Faith? Briefly speaking, it is threefold. First, it is upright, having right thoughts of the eternal. Second, it is profound, rejoicing to study everything that is good and to practise it. Third, it is greatly pitiful, anxious to deliver all living beings from their sorrow.

Question 8: Formerly you said that all the universe was but one state and that the natures of the gods were not different from that of men, so how is it that it is not only by the study of the Eternal and by practice of all kinds of goodness that one reaches that state?

Answer: Man's nature is like a great precious stone. It is bright and pure, but there is the dross of the quarry on it. If men think only of its precious nature, and do not use various means to cleanse it, it will never be pure. Thus, is it with mankind. The nature of the eternal in them is absolute purity, but it is defiled with infinite dross. If men only think of the eternal, and do not use various means to improve their nature, they also will never get pure, because there is infinite dross pervading everything. The practice of all sorts of good is in order to purge away the dross. If men practise all sorts of good, they will naturally fall in with the eternal way.

(c) Briefly speaking, the means are of four kinds:

(i) Cultivate the root of things, by looking on the true nature of all things as eternal, without beginning, independent of man's conception of things, and not permanent in temporary life; by looking on all things linked together by a never-failing law of deeds and their consequences; by nourishing a great pity and cultivating virtue joyfully; by seeking to save all men, not resting in the *nirvana* of the two lower schools, as that which does nothing, for the Eternal Archetype never rests.

(ii) Cease from evil. It is by contrition and repentance that one is enabled to cease from all evil and prevent its increase. As one follows the Eternal Nature he departs from all evil.

(iii) Grow in goodness. It is by diligently honouring and supporting the Three Precious Ones, praising them, rejoicing in their good deeds, and by seeking instructions of the Enlightened. As there is love and respect for the holy character of the Three Precious Ones, faith grows and one desires to get the highest truth.

Besides the influence of God, there is that of His law throughout the universe, and that of the priesthood, the teachers of this law, by which one is able to remove the hindrances to goodness and be firmly rooted in it; for one follows and obeys eternal law and leaves mad hindrances far behind.

(iv) Seek the Eternal's wish. It is an ever-growing desire to save all living beings without exception, so that all may reach the Supreme *nirvana* (Rest) of the Higher Faith, where one follows and obeys the nature of the Eternal for ever. The Eternal nature is vast and pervading all living beings without distinction of this, that, or the other, and is the final rest of all.

(d) As an intelligent saint (Bodhisattva), thus, progresses in religion, he begins to comprehend a little of the Eternal state. As he comprehends the Eternal, he discovers that the Eternal has made eight kinds of sacrifices for men. He descends from his heaven of ease. He becomes incarnate and mingles with less fortunate beings. He grows in the womb of obscurity. He becomes well-known. He sacrifices all other interests, even his home, and becomes a priest devoted to the Eternal. He knows true religion. He preaches the law of the Eternal. He enters the true *nirvana* of perfect peace.

But this intelligent saint (Bodhisattva) is not called the divine eternal embodiment. As in the innumerable ages of the past there still remain some deeds which he has not been able to free entirely from defilement, so there are sufferings corresponding to them in his circumstances, but he is not bound by these imperfections any longer.

(e) Since he is free by the power of the Great Eternal to save men, the Sutra says if we speak of the Bodhisattva going down to some evil place he is not really degraded thereby. It is only in the beginning that it appears so, and, therefore, he descends to strengthen some who are hesitating in fear.

(f) Moreover, the saint from the beginning of his perfect faith is far from having any weakness, and never has any fear of falling back to the state of the two lower schools. Even if he hears that *nirvana* cannot be obtained till after patient toil through troubles lasting for immeasurable and endless *kalpas* of longest durations, still he faints not, as by faith he knows that behind all existence there is naturally the supreme *nirvana* (Rest).

2. Growth in intelligent practice. One must know that there must be growth. When the Bodhisattvas, who from the first follow the correct faith, are about to complete the first term of long *kalpas*, they then fully comprehend the Eternal. It is in a state of complete independence of all form, and they practise those five divine exercise (*Paramitas*) by means of which they pass into the supreme *nirvana*. (1) As they learn that the Eternal has no selfishness, they then follow obediently the practice of all kinds of divine charity. (2) As they learn that the Eternal is undefiled, free from the sins arising from the longings of the five senses, they obediently practise divine perseverance. (3) As they learn that the Eternal is all-enduring, they obediently practise divine endurance. (4) As they learn that the Eternal is ever clear, without confusion, they obediently practise divine unchangeableness. (5) As they learn

that the Eternal is all intelligence, free from ignorance, they obediently practise divine wisdom or judgements.

3. Growth in attainments. This covers the ground from the beginning of the holy pure state up to the highest attainments of sainthood (Bodhisattvahood). What attainments are these? They are those of the Eternal. According to the perception of the senses, this would be called the objective world, but in our present attainment there is nothing outward but the eternal wisdom which is called the Divine Body.

(a) These Bodhisattvas in an instant are able to reach all space throughout all the universe, adoring all the enlightened gods (Buddhas), and requesting them to explain the Eternal Law for the sole purpose of teaching and benefiting all living beings, so as to get the spirit of the Law and not mere fine words. These saints sometimes hurry over various stages of progress so as to get right enlightenment speedily in order to help the weak; sometimes, after a term of countless long *kalpas*, they may become Buddhas in order to encourage the weary ones, and, thus, show by countless ways how to attain Buddha-hood. In reality, as the root of the nature of the seed of sainthood is the same, the growth is the same and the attainment is the same, namely, through the Eternal way. There is no such thing as omitting any term, as all the saints must go through the three terms, though they follow different ways with different men. As men's nature, desires, and dispositions are different, the saints use different methods for their salvation.

(b) Here the growth of this state of sainthood is threefold and is very necessary. The first is that of the true soul, which in no way differs from the Eternal. The second is that of the different means employed to meet the needs of all beings. The third is that of his conceptions of things, where still linger a few false notions disturbing him.

(c) Then comes the holy perfection in all virtues at the head of the world of form, showing themselves as the greatest of mortals. In a moment they correspond exactly to the Eternal Wisdom, and all ignorance being entirely gone, this correspondence is called the root seed of all wisdom. These saints naturally possess powers beyond all thought, able to manifest themselves throughout all points of space for the good of all beings.

Question 9: As space in infinite, worlds are infinite. As worlds are infinite, living beings are infinite. As living beings are infinite, the differences of thought in them are infinite, and in such a state their respective magnitudes cannot be determined, none can know or explain them. If ignorance is removed, then no vain guesses will exist. How can we understand that which is called the seed of wisdom?

Answer: All the universe originally was only One Soul needing not to conjecture at things. As living beings only imperfectly see the world outside them, their minds are limited and they begin to make ideal conjectures different from the reality, thus, preventing a right understanding of things. All the Buddhas and *Tathagatas* (Incarnate Models) are independent of the senses, and omniscient. The real soul is the nature of all things. This soul shines forth on all minds. I has great wisdom in innumerable ways, according to the different needs of men, so as to instruct them in all kinds of ways. On this account it has been named the seed of all wisdom.

Question 10: If the Buddhas have a natural power to manifest themselves everywhere for the good of all living beings, and if all beings see their manifested bodies, then men observe their various modifications; and if they hear their words, which are good, how do you say that most people cannot see them?

Answer: The divine nature of the Buddhas and of the *Tathagata* is one pervading all space without any effort of the mind, therefore, we say it is natural, yet depending on men for its manifestation. The soul of living beings is just like a mirror. If it is not clear it cannot reflect. So if the soul of living beings is not pure, the divine nature cannot be properly reflected.

CHAPTER 4

The Practice of the Mahayana Faith

Having illustrated the principles, we now discuss the practice of them. This is one account of those who have not entered the ranks of the upright ones, and so we explain the practice of Faith. What Faith? What practice? Briefly speaking, faith is of four kinds. First, belief in the root of all things—that is, rejoicing to think of God, the True Reality. Second, belief in the infinite merits of divinity (Buddhahood), ever thinking of it drawing near to it, supporting and adoring it, growing in goodness, and seeking all wisdom from it. Third, belief in the great benefit of the Law, always thinking how to practise all the different means of salvation. Fourth, belief in the Priesthood's ability to cultivate the right doctrine; having themselves found good, they help others to obtain it; ever rejoicing to approach all the saints, and seeking to learn and practise the truth as it is in the Eternal.

To realise the faith, practice consists of five stages. These five are:

1. The stage of charity.
2. The stage of holiness.
3. The stage of enduring wrong.
4. The stage of perseverance.
5. The stage of preventing vain thoughts, and the practice of divine wisdom or judgements.

A. How to practise the state of charity. If one sees any coming to beg in their need, money should be given them according to one's ability in order to prevent covetousness in oneself and to make the poor glad. If one sees men in trouble, fear, and danger, the fear should be relieved according to one's power. If men come to inquire about religion, on should explain the various means according to one's ability. In all things one should not seek the honours of fame or wealth, but, simply feeling that having received benefit oneself, one should impart the same benefit to others, so that they may return to true wisdom.

B. How to practise the state of holiness. This is to observe the Ten Commandments:

1. Thou shalt not kill anything.
2. Thou shalt not steal.
3. Thou shalt not commit adultery.
4. Thou shalt not be doublefaced.
5. Thou shalt not curse.
6. Thou shalt not lie.

7. Thou shalt not speak vanity.
8. Thou shalt keep far from coveting.
9. Thou shalt not insult, deceive, flatter, or trick.
10. Thou shalt be free from anger and heresy.

As for the priests, in order to overcome the temptations of the world they should keep far from the stir of the world and ever live in quietness, cultivating few desires and satisfaction with their lot, while mortifications should take place after committing the smallest sin. Their hearts must be moved with fear and most sincere repentance, and in no way must they regard the prohibitions of the *Tathagata* lightly. They should also guard against appearances of evil, lest men should commit the sin of speaking evil against the priesthood.

C. How to practise the state of bearing the cross (enduring wrong). This is what is called the duty of enduring the aspersions of others without a feeling of revenge through the eight storms of life. That is, to be the same in prosperity, in adversity, in honour and dishonour, in good and evil report, in trouble and in joy.

D. How to practise the state of perseverance. The heart must be never weary in well-doing of all sorts, having a purpose firm and strong, far from any weakness. Thinking of having passed in vain through all the great sorrows of mind and body down through past ages without doing any good is sad; to advance in the scale of being one should diligently practise all sorts of good. Having obtained good oneself, one should make this known to others, so as to speedily leave all sorrow.

Next, although some men practise faith, yet, as from former generations they had many grave sins and delusions, they are troubled by all sorts of evil spirits, or are bound by all sorts of affairs of the world, or are troubled with sickness or with many other trials; they must, therefore, have courage and diligence, and worship God (Buddha) night and day at all the appointed times, repent with all sincerity, seek light from Buddha, rejoice with others' good so as to return towards true wisdom. This should be done constantly without intermission, so as to escape from all delusions and to grow in all goodness.

E. How to practise the state of checking idle thought and of cultivating sound judgement. To check idle thought is to cease from being misled by impressions and to follow and obey the rules. To reflect is to differentiate between the different laws of temporary existence and to obey the rules of sound judgement. How are these to be followed? These two states are to be gradually cultivated, not independently, but simultaneously.

1. As to the practice of checking vain thoughts, it should be done in a quiet place, properly seated and in a proper spirit. It is not the practice of breathing air in a special manner into the body, as is the custom of some religions, thinking thereby

to get the vital spirit of nature into the body, nor the use of anything that has form or colour, whether of empty space or of the four elements earth, water, fire, and wind, or even of the knowledge gained by any experience of the senses, for all kinds of ideas as soon as thought of must be put away, even the idea of banishing them must also be put away. As all existence originally came to be without any idea of its own, it ceases to be also without any idea of its own; any thoughts arising, therefore, must be from being absolutely passive. Nor must one follow the mind in its excursions to everything outsides itself and then chase that thought away. If the mind wanders far away, it must be brought back into its proper state. One should know that the proper state is that of the soul alone without anything outside of it. Again, even this soul has no form and no thought by which we can conceive of it properly.

(a) Having risen from the sitting posture, whether in going out or coming in, or in any work, at all times one should think of the means of checking vain thoughts, and should examine whether he succeeds in it or whether he follows them. In time one gets perfect in the practice and the mind is at rest. As the mind is at rest it gradually gets courage to proceed; in this way it reaches the peace of the Eternal, far beyond all trouble with faith, increasing so that it will soon be so perfect as never to fail anymore. But doubters, unbelievers, blasphemers, great sinners, those who are conceited, who will not persevere, and such-like people, cannot obtain this peace of the Eternal.

(b) Note next that by this peace one knows that in the spiritual world the peace of the spiritual bodies of all the Buddhas and of all living bodies is one and the same, and is called the divine peace. Know that the root of this peace is in the Eternal. If this is continued, there gradually arises in the mind an infinite peace.

(c) If there should be some men without the strength which come from good deeds who are troubled with evil spirits and the gods and demons of outside religions, appearing sometimes in ugly forms, causing fear to them whilst sitting in contemplation, at other times appearing in lovely forms to tempt them, they should think of the One Eternal Soul, then these appearances will vanish and give no more trouble. These evil spirits, whether taking the form of the heavenly beings, of Bodhisattvas, or of the *Tathagata*, all full of perfection, or using magic formulae, or preaching charity, morality, endurance of wrong, perseverance, contemplation, wisdom, or discussing the one unseen reality, the formless reality, the passionless reality, without enmity and without love, without cause and without effect—nothing but pure emptiness—say that this is the true *nirvana*! They also teach men how to know the past and to know the future, and how to know what is in the mind of others, and how to have unfailing gifts of speech, causing men to covet the fame and wealth of this world.

Or, again, these evil spirits cause men to be frequently violently angry or very happy, without anything to steady them; sometimes to have great compassion, or to be sleepy or ill, or to be without perseverance; or they cause men to persevere for a time and then to fall back worse than ever, to lose faith, to have many doubts and fears, or give up their practice of checking vain thoughts and make them follow miscellaneous matters and be chained by the many affairs of the world, so as to give men a certain kind of peace, somewhat similar to the true peace, but which is the product of outside religions and not the true peace of the Eternal.

Or, again, these evil spirits cause men for one, two, three, or even seven days, to remain in contemplation, as if enjoying delicious food; they are most happy in mind and body without any hunger or thirst; or they may be led to eat without any control, sometimes much and sometimes little, so that the countenance changes, and exhibits gladness or sorrow accordingly.

As there are such things, religious people should always wisely examine themselves, lest their minds should fall into the nets of heresy. They should carefully rectify their thoughts and neither adopt nor be attached to them, but keep themselves far from all delusions.

One should know that the peace of outside religions is of the senses, of the affections, to gratify self, desiring the honours of fame and the wealth of the world.

But the true peace is not in the realms of the senses or in possessions, and even after contemplation there is neither the feeling of having attained perfection with no further effort, nor conceit for what has been accomplished. All trials gradually diminish.

If men do not cultivate this peace, there is not other way to get the seed of the *Tathagata*, the Incarnate Lord.

As the peace of this world mostly arises from the pleasure which is given to the senses, it is bound to the three worlds of form, of desire, and of no-form, like that of the outside religions. Once men leave the guidance of sound wisdom, false doctrines at once arise.

(d) Next note that those who diligently set their minds on securing this peace, should, in the present generation, obtain ten advantages:

(i) All the Buddhas and Bodhisattvas throughout all space always protect them.

(ii) None of the evil spirits can cause them any fear.

(iii) They cannot be deceived by any of the ninety-five kinds of outside religions.

(iv) They are far beyond questioning the deep things of the Buddhist religion, and great sins gradually diminish.

(v) There is an end to all doubts and all kinds of heresies.

(vi) Faith in the world of the *Tathagata* (God Incarnate) grows.

(vii) They leave sorrow far behind in the minds of mortals, while they themselves have no fear.

(viii) Their spirits become gentle and peaceable, they put off pride and conceit, and are not troubled by other people's opinions.

(ix) Although they have not obtained full peace at all times and in every place, they are able to lessen their trials, and do not covet the world's pleasures.

(x) When their peace is secured, they are unmoved by any seductions of outside attractions.

2. Now, if men practise only contemplation, the mind is damped, or gets weary, and does not rejoice in all goodness, but is far from pity; therefore, it is necessary to cultivate reasoning or reflection.

(a) One should reflect that nothing made throughout the universe can last long; in a moment it may be destroyed.

(b) One should reflect that all thought rises and vanishes again like a wave, and is, therefore, a sorrow.

(c) One should reflect that all the past is misty like a dream, that all the present is like lightning, that all the future rises suddenly like a cloud in the sky.

(d) One should reflect that the bodies of all living

beings are unclean, full of all kinds of uncleanness, and, therefore, not to be rejoiced in.

(e) Thus, one should reflect that all living beings, from eternity down the ages, being influenced by ignorance, live and die and endure all the great sorrows of mind and body; and reflect on the endless trials of the present and on the immeasurable sorrows of the future, which cannot be got rid of and which men are scarcely aware of. When all men's lives are so full of sorrow, they are greatly to be pitied.

(f) Having thought of these things, one should stir oneself up to make a Great vow to lead one's own soul to leave the finite and gain the infinite, cultivate every means of grace to deliver all men for ever from their sorrows and obtain the highest joys of *nirvana*.

(g) Having made this great vow, one must not give up practising it or be weary in it, but at all times and all places engages in every good that is in one's power.

3. Whilst sitting in meditation, one's mind should be bent on checking vain thoughts. At other times one should reflect carefully in regard to everything whether it should or should not be done. Whether walking or resting, lying down or rising up, both reflecting and checking vain thoughts should go together. This is what is meant by the saying that although we practise all these things, our perfection is not really produced by ourselves, but by the nature of the Eternal working through us.

Again, thinking of the never-failing law of cause and effect, and joy and sorrow as the reward of good and evil, when we think of law we must also think of this goal so difficult to attain.

The practice of checking vain thoughts is to sever attachment to the world, and to put away the fears and weaknesses of the two lower schools of Buddhism.

The practice of reflection is to deliver from the narrow sin of the two lower schools, who do not have the vow of great pity for others, and who do not keep far from ordinary men who do not practise goodness.

In this way the two methods of reflection and the checking of vain thoughts are mutually helpful to one another and inseparable. If both are not practised, one cannot then enter on the way of wisdom.

4. Next consider those who begin to learn the five methods of this chapter, (p. 48), and desire to get right faith, but are timid and weak. As they live in this world of extreme suffering, they fear they cannot constantly approach God (Buddha) and personally contribute to His service. Thus, they fear they cannot attain to this perfect faith, and have a mind to renounce their search after it.

These should know that the *Tathagata* has most excellent means to strengthen their faith. It is by having the mind set only on the things of God (Buddha), and by desiring that one may be born in another world of Buddha and be constantly with

Him forever, far from all evil, that one may attain this end. As the Sutra says, if a man sets his mind to think only of God (the Amitabha Buddha), who is in the happiest realm of the West (paradise), and if his good deeds are in the right direction, and if he desires to get to that happy Paradise, he will then get there; and as he is always in the presence of Buddha, he will never fall back.

If we reflect on the eternal nature of God (the Amitabha Buddha), and constantly practise this method, we will in the end reach the place of true wisdom.

CHAPTER 5

The Advantages of the Practice of the Mahayana Faith

Having discussed the practice of these principles we will now discuss the advantages of practising them. We have already given a general idea of the mysterious resources of the Buddhas of the Mahayana School.

A. If any one desires to get a right faith in the deep things of the *Tathagata*, and desires to be far from error, which brings religion into disrepute, and get the Mahayana Faith, he should lay hold of this book, study it and practise it. In the end he will attain to the very highest truth.

B. If a man listens to this truth, and has neither fear nor weakness, such a man is certain to succeed to the rank of Buddha, and to be enrolled as such by all the Divine Ones.

C. If a man should be able to reform all living beings throughout all the systems in the universe, in order to make them good, he would not be equal to a man who, for only the time he takes to eat a meal, studies this way of deliverance. The two methods are incomparable.

D. Next, if a man takes this book, studies and practises it only for a day and a night, the blessings received would be incalculable. Even if all the Buddhas of the universe were each to speak of these blessings for incalculably and immeasurably long *kalpas*, they could not exhaust them, for the blessings of the Eternal Nature are endless, and the blessings to this man would be also in like manner endless.

E. But if there should be any who speak evil and do not believe in this book, the recompense of their sin will be to suffer immense pain for measureless ages. On this account all men should respectfully believe and not speak evil of it, thereby injuring themselves more and more and others too, destroying every hope of deliverance by destroying the Eternal Soul of the Three Precious Ones originally in man (the soul of the universe, the body of laws pervading the universe, the body of men teaching these laws), for all the Divine Ones attain to *nirvana* by this means, and all the saints attain Buddha-wisdom by the same practice.

F. Know that it is by this means that the Bodhisattvas of the past obtained pure faith, and that it is by this means that the Bodhisattvas of the present obtain pure faith, therefore, it is by this means that the Bodhisattvas of the future must obtain pure faith. Thus, all men should diligently study and practise it.

The Closing Hymn

Deep and wide is Buddhist Law,
This in brief I have declared;
Godward are eternal stores,
Blessings give to countless worlds!

TRANSLATOR'S SUPPLEMENTARY

The Great Physician's Twelve Desires (Vows)

NOTE

The first Buddhist temple in or around Nara in Japan was built by Koreans, at the invitation of the Japanese rulers in the sixth century of the Christian era.

One of the most remarkable sights I have seen in Japan is a temple at Horiyuji, near Nara, to the Great Physician (Yakushi they call him). It is filled with innumerable votive offerings, to show that the sick were healed by prayers to him. The zeal of modern Christian scientists is far more than eclipsed by this wonderful record of fifteen centuries there.

By bringing the highest ideals of the East and the West together for comparison, it is hoped that special attention should be called to this rather than to the failings and low practices of either East or West.

The Scripture which describes this Great

Physician has one very striking passage on his Twelve Vows or Purpose in coming to the world. These Twelve Vows I translate below:

1. I come from heaven with the highest wisdom to shine on infinite innumerable worlds accompanied by thirty-two great angels, different forms of Kwanyin, and glorious legions, it will be for the purpose of delivering all beings, to be godlike like myself.
2. I come with my body within and without pure as crystal, without a flaw, with great light and profound virtue living in peace with a glory surpassing that of sun and moon, it will be to enlighten all who are living in darkness.
3. I come again with wisdom bringing infinite knowledge and goodness so that no living creature may suffer from any want but have all they need.
4. I come in order that those who are in evil ways may find peace in the way of wisdom, and in order that those who only know the old Buddhism, may know the new Buddhism.
5. I come in order that the multitudes who study religion may discover the perfect way, and if they have erred on hearing my name may be delivered from hell, and also attain to holiness.
6. I come so that all beings who are cripples, ugly and foolish, blind, deaf and dumb,

hunchback, leprous and mad, and all sorts of suffering, on hearing my name may be healed of all their diseases.

7. I come so that the incurables, the homeless, those without doctors or medicine, without friends or relatives, the poor and the sorrowful, on hearing my name shall be delivered from all their troubles and live in peace of mind and body, have their families flourish in abundance and attain the highest wisdom.
8. I come so that women driven by all sorts of trials to hate their lives, and no longer desire to be women, on hearing my name may be changed to men, and attain the highest wisdom.
9. I come so that those who are in the bonds of evil spirits, or of heresies fallen into all sorts of evil, on hearing my name may be led to right knowledge, and gradually practise goodness and attain to the highest wisdom.
10. I come so that those who have fallen to the clutches of the law, are bound and beaten and imprisoned, or are about to be executed or have endless calamities, insults, sorrows burning both body and soul, on hearing my name may secure my grace and power, and be delivered from all their sorrows.
11. I come so that those driven by hunger and thirst to do wrong, on hearing my name shall be fed and satisfied with wisdom and find perfect rest.

12. I come so that all the poor and naked, and those suffering from heat and cold, and divers flies and secret creepers night and day, on hearing my name may turn to practise religion, according to their bent, will receive the garments of highest wisdom, glorious treasures and best music, and be fully satisfied with all.

* * *

The Creed of Half Asia

To Sin King

This creed deserves to rank among the sublimest literary productions of the human mind, from Job to Kant, together with those of the best thinkers of India and China.

Many devout people of the Confucian and Taoist schools, as well as Buddhists, recite it daily just as Christians sing a choice hymn.

It states the solid fundamental principles of religion which commend themselves, not merely to the majority of Asiatics, but also to the majority of men universally. It includes the need of Divine Power to save men, the great Atonement, Divine Inspiration, Divinest Miracles, past, present, and to come, and Immortality.

When this best Eastern thought is united to the best Western thought, whatever may be deficient in definition in either singly, may meet the approval of that conscience which God has given to mankind collectively.

The creed is as follows:

Hail self-existent illuminator. Who in exercising deepest Wisdom seest the unreality of all that is reached by the five senses, and canst save from all troubles and dangers.

O Sariputra (The Divine Seed?), the Manifested is not different from the Eternal, and the Eternal is not different from the Manifested. Thought and Action are also, thus, mutually related.

The Divine Seed (?) is the Eternal in all laws of the Universe. He was never born, nor will ever die.

He is neither clean nor unclean, is neither added to nor subtracted from. He is without sorrow, and will not perish. He is without acquired Wisdom, because he has received none.

The Illuminators depending on this Eternal Wisdom are without anxiety. Having no anxiety, they have no fear and are far from impossible dreams and thoughts. They are eventually immortals.

All the Illuminated past, present, and to come, depending on this Divine Wisdom, obtain the Highest Wisdom.

Therefore, know that this Divine Wisdom is a great Divine Magic, a great brilliant magic, the greatest magic, and a magic without a peer.

It can deliver you from all kinds of troubles. This is a real truth without any falsehood. Therefore, in repeating this magic incantation, sum up and say:

Praise, Praise,

Praise God,
Praise His eternal wisdom (Law)
Praise the students of this Law
The illumined!

(Translated from the Buddhist Tripitaka, Nanjio's Catalogue, no. 20.)

Select Bibliography*

The Christian Legend of Barlaam and Josaphat has been mentioned in the Introduction to this volume. Details of the Loeb edition (Oxford University Press) are: St. John Damascene: *Barlaam and Ioasaph,* translated by the Rev. G.R. Woodward . . . and Harold Mattingly (third impression, revised). An abbreviated form of the legend, though still lengthy, appears in *The Golden Legend* of Jacobus de Voragine (born AD 1230); or, to give the work its original title: *Historia Longobardica seu Legenda Sanctorum.* Caxton published his translation in 1483. Wynkyn de Worde issued an edition during 1493, followed by further editions later. The Kelmscott Press issued an edition in 1892. The Caxton text, in modernised spelling, is given complete in *Leaves from the Golden Legend.* Chosen by H.D. Madge,

*It is felt that a short selection from the many scholarly works on Buddhism may be helpful to those wishing to make a further study of the Mahayana. The following list, though brief, contains what the editor considers some of the most important works.

LL.M., London, Archibald Constable & Co. Ltd., 1907 (pp. 27-51 inclusive).

Conze, Edward, *Buddhist Scriptures,* selected and translated by Edward Conze, Harmondsworth, Penguin Books (Penguin Classics, edited by E.V. Rieu), 1959. An important selection, excellently arranged, and with a scholarly commentary by Dr. Conze.

—, *Selected Sayings from the Perfection of Wisdom* (the *Prajnaparamita*), London, The Buddhist Society, 1955.

David-Neel, Alexandra, and Lama Yongden, *The Secret Oral Teachings in Tibetan Buddhist Sects,* Calcutta, Maha Bodhi Society of India, n. d. (The English translation from the French original was made by Captain H.N.M. Hardy.)

The Diamond Sutra, translated by A.F. Price, with a Foreword by Dr. W.Y. Evans-Wentz. The notes are also useful, London, The Buddhist Society, 1947 (sec. edn.,1955).

Eliade, Mircea, *Yoga: Immortality and Freedom,* translated from the French by Willard R. Trask. London, Routledge & Kegan Paul, 1958 (original title in French: *Le Yoga. Immortalité et Liberté,* Paris, Payot, 1954). Copyright, New York, the Bollingen Foundation Inc., 1958. This monumental volume by a former lecturer from the Sorbonne, who is now professor of the history of religion at the University of Chicago, will be found invaluable by those who wish to carry their studies further. It covers not only the Yoga of Patanjali, but also

Mahayana Yoga, Oriental alchemy, and mystical eroticism. The annotations are extensive, and the bibliography extremely full and useful. The index, likewise, is lengthy and detailed.

Evans-Wentz, W.Y., *Tibet's Great Yogi Milarepa*: A Biography from the Tibetan, being the *Jetsun-Kahbum* . . . according to the late Lama Kazi Dawasamdup's English rendering, edited with Introduction and Annotations, London, Oxford University Press, 1928, sec. edn., 1951.

—, *The Tibetan Book of the Dead*, with a psychological commentary by Dr. C.G. Jung, Introducing Foreword by Lama Anagarika Govinda, and Foreword by Sir John Woodruffe, London, Oxford University Press, 1927, second impression, 1936 (sec. edn., 1949, with a second impression, 1951; third edn., 1957).

—, *Tibetan Yoga and Secret Doctrines*, or Seven Books of Wisdom of the Great Path, etc. Arranged and edited with Introductions and Annotations to serve as a commentary. Foreword by Dr. R.R. Marett, London, Oxford University Press, 1935 (sec. edn. with yogic commentary by translator Chen-Chi Chang, 1958).

—, *The Tibetan Book of the Great Liberation* or the Method of Realising Nirvana through Knowing the Mind, etc. Introductions, Annotations, etc., as for the previous volumes. Psychological commentary by Dr. C.G. Jung, London, Oxford University Press, 1954. This volume is of considerable interest for those who read Ashvaghosha, and its extremely lengthy and detailed General

Introduction is essential for those who would pursue the further study of the Mahayana. All of Dr. Evans-Wentz's volumes contain copious explanatory notes and long introductions, and he has an amazing facility in making difficult and even abstruse aspects of this religion remarkably easy to understand. The importance of these four volumes cannot be overestimated.

Govinda, Lama Anagarika, *Foundation of Tibetan Mysticism* (translated from the German by the author), London, Rider & Company, 1959. Another scholastic work of the highest importance.

—, *The Psychological Attitude of Early Buddhist Philosophy,* London, Rider & Company, 1960. This work summarizes Pali Buddhism, and is also a gradual and logical approach to the Mahayana and Tantricism, dealing, at the same time, with the interrelatedness and non-substantiality of the phenomena. It was originally published in India, and this is the first edition to be easily available in Europe.

Humphreys, Christmas, *Buddhism,* Harmondsworth, Penguin Books (Pelican Books), 1951 (and several reprints). A very useful book for the general reader, and an introduction for those wishing to make further studies.

Johnson, Raynor C., *The Imprisoned Splendour*, London, Hodder & Stoughton, 1953 (fifth impression 1958), A valuable work of reading in conjunction with others in the above list (see also under *Buddhism* in its Index). Its subtitle is: An

Approach to Reality, based upon the significance of data drawn from the fields of Natural Science, Psychical Research and Mystical Experience. The author's strict scientific training (he is an adherent of the unified-field theory) and rigid methodology place him above any suspicion.

The Lankavatara Sutra, a Mahayana text translated for the first time by Daisetz Teitaro Suzuki, London, Routledge & Kegan Paul Ltd., 1932 (reprinted 1956). The very lengthy Introduction to this volume is worth careful study.

Patanjali, *How to Know God: The Yoga Aphorisms of Patanjali*, translated with a new commentary by Swami Prabhavananda and Christopher Isherwood, London, George Allen & Unwin, Ltd., 1953. One of the best and most readable translations of a classic guide to the spiritual life. The commentary is amazingly lucid. Although not directly connected with the subject of the present work, the book is important, and an indispensable companion to any of the volumes listed above.

Suzuki, B.L., *Mahayana Buddhism*, with an Introduction by Prof. D.T. Suzuki, and a Foreword by Christmas Humphreys, London, George Allen & Unwin, 1959 (originally published by the Buddhist Society, London, 1939; sec. enl. edn., London, David Marlowe, 1948).

Suzuki, D.T., *Mysticism, Christian and Buddhist*, London, George Allen & Unwin Ltd., 1957.

Zürcher, E., *The Buddhist Conquest of China: The Spread and Adaptation of Buddhism in Early*

Mediaeval China, Leiden, E.J. Brill, 1959. (Sinica Leidensia, Institutum Sinologicum Lugduno-Batavum, vol. XI)—2 vols.: vol. 1—Text; vol. 2—Notes, Bibliography, and Indices. The first attempt to describe in a Western language the formative phase of Buddhism in China, from the middle of the first century AD to the early part of the fifth century AD. Of considerable Interest for the scholar, this work is not easy reading for the general reader first approaching the subject.